COURAGE OVER ADVERSITY

....

A JOURNEY OUT
OF THE OCCULT

ANGIE AMUSO

Transforming Books
Adelaide, South Australia

Copyright © 2016 by Angie Amuso.

All rights reserved. No part of this publication may be reproduced, distributed or transmitted in any form or by any means, including photocopying, recording, or other electronic or mechanical methods, without the prior written permission of the publisher, except in the case of brief quotations embodied in critical reviews and certain other noncommercial uses permitted by copyright law. For permission requests, write to the publisher at the address below.

Transforming Books
www.transformingbooks.com
info@transformingbooks.com

Publisher's Note: This is a work of nonfiction. Some names have been changed to protect the privacy of those involved.

Scriptures taken from the Holy Bible, New International Version®, NIV®. Copyright © 1973, 1978, 1984, 2011 by Biblica, Inc.™ Used by permission of Zondervan. All rights reserved worldwide. www.zondervan.com The "NIV" and "New International Version" are trademarks registered in the United States Patent and Trademark Office by Biblica, Inc.™

A CIP catalogue record for this book is available from the National Library of Australia

Courage Over Adversity ~ A Journey out of the Occult/ Angie Amuso. -- 1st ed.
ISBN 978-0-9953659-0-2

About the Cover Artist

Sarah Rowan Dahl is a pioneering creative force. The American born, mother of two moved to Sydney shortly after graduation from Converse College in 2003. Obtaining a BFA in Studio Art, she has big dreams and an inspiring faith. Sarah is a performance painter, who paints live in front of audiences, bringing a creative experience to events, from corporate to festivals, weddings, pubs and churches. One of her main goals as an artist is to help raise over a million dollars to help end human trafficking.

www.sarahrowandahl.com

We are called to be spiritual beings, not necessarily human beings. This is why most people are seeking the spiritual things of this world which are accompanied by the supernatural. Unfortunately the occult is a counterfeit and deceives us from having a relationship with our Creator through the Holy Spirit. In her book "Courage over Adversity" Angie writes from the heart of her own experience of how she came out of the deepest, darkest pit into the light of the Glory of the one true God. This book will encourage many who are on a similar journey.
– Adam F Thompson
Author
www.voiceoffireministries.org

This is a compelling book of breakthrough in spite of setbacks through family matters, health, abuse, faith and spirituality. This testimony of Angie's will build faith and hope into the path of love, healing and purpose. These are heartfelt truths, some of which are not often told, to empower others to step into their greatness and live a life with grace, purpose and joy.
– Julie-Anne Powell
Director – Liebusters Australasia

The most apparent need for the Body of Christ in this day and age is learning how to hear the voice of Christ amidst all the other voices. Angie Amuso's book, Courage Over Adversity, answers those questions beautifully. I have enjoyed and marveled reading page after page and encourage each person, young or old, to read this book and pass it on to others. Her captivating story of human frailty and despair being overcome with His unspoken courage. Each wave of darkness being overtaken by waves of Christ's hope and love. Simply Brilliant!

– Shampa Mom (Teapot)
India

Angie Amuso is an amazing woman of God. She embodies the Spirit of Service and lives like Christ in the earth. She has an amazing story of overcoming adversity and a lifestyle of the occult. After reading her book you too will feel the power and strength rise from Christ within you to enter into his plans for your life.

– Darren Canning
Revival Preacher and Author
darrencanning.com

INTRODUCTION

....

IN SEARCH OF TRUTH

I was a self-professed hippie, wearing vintage clothing and interested in alternative spirituality. I was always into what was different. If you had told me years ago that I would one day chose Jesus as my spiritual pathway, I would have said that you had rocks in your head. It definitely was not part of my plan. In my ignorance, I stumbled into a spiritual realm that encompassed lies and deception. This was a world of darkness that was incapable of any light, any truth, hope or future. I believed my life was over and there was no return. My story, which began in 1998, is one of courage over adversity, of the triumph of truth over lies. I am compelled to write it so that others may be informed of the consequences of such a search journeying into darkness that led me to a spiritual prison. My hope is that it will help others to avoid the heartache and torment

I endured. I aim, too, to inform the Christian community of how and why desperate people often seek truth in the wrong places.

There can be serious consequences if you connect with the supernatural in the wrong places. My journey involved a spiritual hunger which led me into a world of darkness. I thought I was on a pathway to spiritual truth, enlightenment, where all my questions would be answered ~ but some questions will not be answered in this lifetime.

I have changed some of the names of people to protect their privacy, but that is the only part of my story that is not factual.

BUTTERFLY

Have you ever watched a butterfly develop and grow?
It's an experience that is so special that all should know.
It starts as a cocoon so repressed, enclosed, entwined,
There's no indication or vision of what beauty is inside
But when so slowly that butterfly emerges, such knowledge and freedom she'll find.
Struggle, struggle, oh it feels so hard, impossible some of the time.
Wriggle, wriggle, push, desire, yes, head's out, disoriented and a bit blind
Yes, butterfly, you can do it if you believe with your mind.
She sees others watching, encouraging, supporting this growth and development.
She cries for help "Pull this off, it is so hard!" but only love and reassuring words can be sent,
For they have the confidence she will succeed.
This is a process. Courage and patience, one step at a time, is what she needs.
With all that determination and love and support, she pushes and struggles that inch more.

Out pops the beautifully formed, colourful wings, onlookers watch and adore.
What beauty is emerging from this cocoon.
Butterfly freedom, confidence and wisdom she will experience soon.
Push, push, struggle, nearly there,
Yes, she's achieved her ultimate goal and thanks the people who really did care,
Cause without all that encouragement it would have seemed an impossible feat.
Fly, fly beautiful butterfly, fly into the universe, into the sky,
Finally, all the struggle is gone and she's free,
Enjoying life's wonders, not sure where they'll take her,
But living as happy as can be.

PATHWAYS

The pain and confusion and hurt inside,
Has made me go inward, I've run to hide.
For years I've suppressed and hidden my pain
It's like dark clouds and thunderous rain.
So I've looked in my clouded mirror and what did I see?
I have seen what I didn't want it to be.
Acknowledge, accept is the first place to start
And in time I will find forgiveness of heart.
God helps me to be strong so I can stand
So I ask for help from His guiding hand.
You must take the good and learn from the bad
Enjoy the pleasures and deal with the sad,
For I can truly grow and learn from the strife.
And this is what makes me appreciate life,
I hold the lock and I hold the key,
Only I can direct what my pathway will be.
And when I have opened that lock inside
I will no longer have reason to run and hide.
All those dark clouds will disappear
And the rain will wash all those deep, dark fears
And all the hard work that I have done

Will bring blue skies and a penetrating sun.
And I will walk in amazing light,
Tall standing and never again losing sight
Of my true purpose on this earth.

ONE

MY BEGINNING

Maryann and I did everything together. I loved her with a passion. My mum to this day recalls a story of my sister and I being in separate wooden cots sharing the same little purple bedroom. At the age of about one year, Maryann would jump her cot over to mine, mum would come into the room and see Maryann in my cot with her arm around me, comforting me. Maryann was, and still is, a very special gift to me. I believe she was a gift from heaven because He knew the future and knew we would need each other.

I was the first of twin daughters born to an Australian mother and Italian father. My mother tells me that the nurse in the Maternity ward looked at me in the humidicrib and said, 'Please call this one Angela because she looks like an angel!' My twin was named Maryann after mum's mum. Both of us were named after our grandmothers - dad believed that it was important to continue the Italian tradition of honouring previous generations. We both enjoyed a special bond with our big brother who was three years older.

The memories I have of my childhood are an extreme paradox: fond and dark. I learnt from a very young age to hold on tightly to the good memories. Maryann was the 'good' in my world. We grew up in Semaphore Park, Adelaide and our house was two streets walk away from the beach. I loved the beach! I still do to this day. In the daylight hours it was a place I longed to be: playing, swimming, walking and resting. However, night-time was a different experience, as night after night I was troubled by a recurring dream about huge waves flooding our street. In the dream I would be standing at the bus stop directly across from our house, watching the waves come closer and closer, getting higher and higher. I would wait for the waves to rise and take us all out. It scared me. I believe now it spoke of the fear and panic that was happening in my heart. Overwhelming emotions hit me hard as a child - negative emotions, troubled feelings, knowing there was a storm. Life felt dangerous and out of control.

Whilst I was still young, around eight years old, I would regularly tell my sister that there was a spiritual truth that I must connect to. Neither of us understood what that meant but there was a longing a call, a something out there that I had to know about. It felt as though a puzzle was not complete in my heart. I understood in my heart that there was a purpose, something that I had to achieve. It bothered me not really understanding those feelings and my sister would freak out a little when I shared my heart in this way. It was real to me, but didn't make sense to either of us.

My Dad was a Catholic but we never attended church, even though we had all been christened as babies. Our next door neighbours were Pentecostal Christians and our families got along really well. We spent a lot of time with each other and Michelle their youngest child became a best friend to Maryann and I. Michelle's mother, Auntie Marie would lead a Christian group at our school called 'Joy Time', and mum used to help her out. There were lots of games and lollies and I remember it as a good experience for Maryann and I. I liked it most because I got to see my mum.

When Maryann and I were about ten years old, Dad decided that it was time for us to be confirmed into the Catholic church. Early every Sunday morning, for two years, Dad would bang on our bedroom door and yell at us to get out of bed and get ready for church. We dreaded Sunday mornings with a passion. We went, but unwillingly. The church was cold and large; we sat in pews that were as uncomfortable as the atmosphere inside. Each Sunday Dad gave us a few coins to put in the offering box. I was a submissive child, but when the offering box came around I did not want to put my money in it. We were poor, we had little money and it bothered me that I had to put the money in that wooden box. I knew that money was needed for food for our family. I didn't understand it was giving to God. I saw it as giving to this large, cold, scary authority that I did not relate to - it didn't make sense to me. I never kept the money though, I always put it in the box. Maryann felt the same. Maryann and I dreaded the communion experience too. Each week we would walk the line, up the red carpet, patiently and politely waiting for our turn. With dread in our heart we obediently opened our mouth as the Priest stood above us, all dressed in his robes, placing the wafer onto our tongue and speaking something over us. We hated the way the communion wafer stuck to the roof of our mouths, but it was important to Dad so we had to cooperate.

Courage Over Adversity

The other thing about church that I dreaded was the confession. I will never forget my first confession experience. One by one the children that were being confirmed went into this large wooden box that sat in the corner of the church. The silence was deafening; each child would exit the box quietly and sit down on the pews at the front of the alter and say their penance. By the time it was my turn my heart was racing: I was so scared! I was always a nervous kid, and this terrified me. I slowly opened the door and walked towards a stool in the small space, all alone in the box. I looked around, freaking out on the inside and I sat as the priest slid open the little window. It felt like his eyes were peering directly into my soul. We sat side by side, a little window my only perspective of him. I don't know to this day if he saw the fear on my face! A deep voice spoke: 'What are your sins, my child?' I was almost too cold to reply but in my nervousness I made something up, quietly and respectfully answering his question. After my confession the priest gave me my penance and told me I could go. I remember the sense of relief as I returned to my seat. I don't think I said my penance. I just sat there scared and confused. He said 'my child?' I was thinking: 'I don't want him as my dad. I don't really think I believe in this God.' These were the thoughts that ran through my mind as I sat at the altar, thankful that it was all over. I didn't say my penance because I made up my sin just to get out of there. In my heart I was rebelling because I just didn't believe in the process. The authority of the church scared me. It was so large, so cold, so impersonal to me. I was told what to do, and how God thought. In my mind God had a finger pointing at me. I didn't feel safe. He felt distant and I felt tiny.

I can still see the priest in my mind, in his robes, standing in the pulpit. I didn't know what he was talking about, but I understood in no uncertain terms that I was a sinner. Maryann and I did some Bible studies in a small group with a teacher who spoke about Jesus, but I couldn't focus on what she was saying. When I was scared I would escape to a private place in my heart and mind. Whenever I was overwhelmed I would go to that place and block out everything. I lost a lot of my schooling because I was spending time in that place. Even though I always passed into the next grade, I found school difficult. My whole world was difficult. Family life was stressful, mum didn't like dad and dad didn't like mum. I was terrified of dad. I was waiting for dad to get his gun and kill us. I lived in that space, in that fear as a child. I never dared to speak about that fear, not even to Maryann, however that fear was truly embedded into my heart. It was my reality.

One day, dad took out his gun and locked himself in his bedroom, threatening to take his life. Maryann and I were quickly ushered out of the house. My fear was real. I knew he had the potential to kill with that gun. I was terrified. I was relieved to hear dad didn't take his life, however his actions led him into the psychiatric ward, and a diagnosis: schizophrenia. Mum was called into the hospital and the doctors talked to her about his illness. We visited once and once was enough. My memory is of dad lying in the hospital bed unable to talk. We asked him how he was but he couldn't answer. It distressed Maryann and I greatly. What was wrong with dad? The nurse told us that sometimes medication can do that. We were whisked away and we never went back. In my heart I told my dad I loved him and that I was scared for him. I was glad he was alive, but now I was more scared of him than ever.

It was at this time - I would have been about seven - I called out to God: 'Please help me!' I would kneel by my bed knowing there was more to life than what I was experiencing. I begged Him to help me, if He was real. I knew He could intervene in our crazy world. I didn't hear him speak back, there seemed to be a chasm, unspeakable distance, between Him and me. I was tiny, insignificant, and He was massive and powerful. I hoped he was kind but my experience taught me differently. The huge church structure and hardline authority were the main truths that filled my subconscious. It was an honest prayer that left my heart, and in faith I believed that He might intervene, that help would come. I had no idea of His plan, I just hoped.

Mum and Dad's marriage was turbulent. They loved us, but the ongoing pain and disfunction of their lives made it difficult for us as a family. I loved both of them deeply and I always felt as though I had to protect my mum, to be good, to not cause her any stress. To be obedient. I knew she couldn't handle a naughty kid, life was already difficult enough. I took responsibility in my heart for my mum while I was still very young. My sister was living on the other side of the pendulum. Her behaviour was naughty, she was frustrated with life. I was withdrawn and she was outspoken. I remember one day – I was about seven - having a cigarette. Mum and dad both smoked and we had easy access to cigarettes. We had been smoking at the park one day and mum and dad confronted us., We were busted! As soon as we were caught, I apologised and backed down when our cover didn't work. Maryann and I were disciplined and then to test us, dad said to us, 'Do you want a smoke? offering mum's packet to us' I was like, 'No way. Are you serious?' Maryann, on the other hand said, 'Yeah!' and went to take the cigarette. She got a left hand across the face. I remember scolding her later: 'How can you be so stupid!' That sums up who we were as twin sisters; one lived on one side of the pendulum and the other swung in the opposite direction.

My parents were so important to me. As a child I needed them desperately. I made a decision as an adult that Mum and Dad will always be honoured and respected in my heart; the values and the foundations that they tried to establish in our lives were good. They did their best. As I processed pain later in life I learnt to hold onto the good, to understand that they were both struggling to cope, that life was difficult for them. I had to trust that they did the best job that they could, with what they were facing in their personal lives.

In media class at high school I found a razor blade. A friend in the class was a 'cutter', and I was intrigued. So I copied him and for the first time I learnt to release pain in another way; I cut my wrist, not real deep, but enough to draw blood. I was surprised that it felt good, the pain helped. It felt as though with each cut, emotional pain was leaving my soul. I cut up my arm while sitting in class to relieve the pain I was feeling. My teacher had no idea. I tried to cover the cuts but Maryann saw it and freaked out. She told Mum and Mum knew something was really wrong. She was so upset that I had hurt myself. She knew that dad and her needed to take this seriously. She told Dad and together they went to a psychiatrist for me to get advice on how to deal with my issues. The initial appointment was for them to go together and then the plan was for me to attend the next appointment and explain myself to the psychiatrist. They came home from that appointment arguing violently. It was loud, it was scary. They stormed into the house announcing that they were getting a divorce. Maryann asked when I was going to see the doctor and Mum said, 'The doctor said it's no wonder our child has issues!' I never did see that doctor.

They separated when I was twelve and eventually divorced. I was convinced the breakdown of the marriage was my fault and I took responsibility for it in my heart. Whenever things went wrong I took the responsibility because I hoped that would take away the pain and prevent a family war. Conflict scared me. It was dangerous. I was always scared that it would get out of control, and many times it did. My taking responsibility rarely worked though because it really wasn't my fault. I longed for peace and reconciliation in our home.

My teenage years were just as difficult. I was still cutting to relieve the pain the practice was embedded in my soul - and I was just going through the motions in school. I found a part time job washing dishes at a local Indian restaurant after school. When I was offered a position as an apprentice chef my parents agreed it was a good opportunity and allowed me to leave school, not long after my parents fully separated and I moved out of home. I was fifteen. It was hard to be loyal to both of them. I loved them equally so it was easier to cope with their impending divorce and their anger when I could get perspective from a distance. The reality is that they both went through a tough time. When there is a divorce each person suffers loss that is unique and individual. Grief can be selfish when it is so personal, especially when you want to walk in freedom. Freedom says you have to face the reality of the hurt and pain and not be in denial. But with grief there is a process, and a lot of the time raw emotions ran rampant in all of us. It created a disconnection. I came to realise that I needed both my parents in my world. I contacted each of both and asked them to respect each other when they were with me because

I loved them equally. Unfortunately they both held on to a lot of painful emotion.

Not long after the divorce my dad found out that he had lung cancer. He'd smoked profusely, always with a rolley in his mouth. He smoked Drum. I found it extremely difficult during visits to my Dad. He knew he was dying of cancer but one time a wooden cross caught my eye. It was new, hung around his neck and it stood out to me. I remember thinking about it though he never explained it to me. During each visit he would grab me and hold me real tight, then he repeated over and over to me: 'I love you, I love you'. He was desperate for me to know that I was loved by him, but I found this hard to handle. Dad had never before shown me this much affection. My heart was not coping with this level of emotional connection. To this day I only have one photo with dad holding me. I was about two years old and there is such fear in my little two-year old face. I feel sad today when I see that photo, however it speaks of the truth of the relationship that should have been, and perhaps was there underneath it all. Dad was trying to make up for sixteen years of lost opportunity. I could not cope with this love. I did not know how to handle it though I could feel the fear in his heart. He knew he was dying and every visit with him was incredibly painful and difficult. I never told him that. I continued to visit dad but only if someone else was with me. My brother mainly. When Dad was finally admitted to palliative care, our visits to him in hospital left me with mixed emotions. My brother was the only one who understood this season and I was so thankful he was there. He was my rock, like a pillar. I could tell he felt a sense of responsibility to care for me emotionally and I cared for him too. We held each other time after time after each visit to the hospital. He would hug me in the elevator as we escaped from the ward and from the pain of watching our dad dying. During one visit Dad begged us to help him die. I was so distressed by this. I explained to him that we could not do it, my brother and I were grateful when the nurses sedated him.

Late one night the call came for all of us to gather at the hospital because Dad wasn't expected to make it through the night. Mum, Maryann and I spent the night there, and Mum sat beside him all night, holding his hand. He looked dreadful and his laboured breathing scared me. With each breath I was thinking, 'Is this it?' I waited all night on the lounge next to Maryann. We were a little distance from his hospital bed waiting for him to breathe his last breath. I was shocked by his death experience and was not prepared for the emotional trauma of having to witness it. In the early hours of the morning, about 6:30am my dad took his last breath. I just froze, my body went cold. I went into shock. I wanted to handle it better on the inside but when it was over, I just ran from the hospital room. My mind went crazy, thoughts flooding my mind as I tried to process what I had just witnessed. It made no sense at all. I just wanted to keep running through the dark halls past all the sleeping patients. One of the nurses grabbed me and took me to a private room where I still tried to process what had just happened. I was inconsolable. I had just watched my Dad die!

My Dad had just died and I felt like the world didn't give a damn. Later, after leaving the hospital I remember driving in the car, my emotions erratic, hearing a Sinead O'Conner song: 'Nothing compares to you'. As we were driving away I looked at the world, at the traffic moving by, routine, life as usual, as if nothing had happened. My thoughts to them were: 'Don't you get it? My dad is gone forever.' My life stopped, dead in its tracks. My life would never be the same again. My dad was dead. My thoughts were hijacked. I felt safer knowing Dad was gone yet at the same time felt intense pain. My heart was divided about how I felt. Was my pain a lie? I loved him deeply, but was so scared of him.

Even in his confessions of love in his last hours, I could not process my response. This experience hit me hard, my grief beyond words. I remember going to my room, wanting to be left by myself, but the truth was I didn't really want to be alone. I cried for hours. Then I felt a pressure on my shoulder and a comfort overcame me. It was powerful, the peace that touched my heart was supernatural and during that experience I stopped crying. I knew it was spiritual. I didn't really know what it was but it comforted me and assured me I was going to be okay. I just knew everything was going to be okay. It released peace in my heart as well as a kind of knowing that Dad was okay, too. I never understood that experience in my head but I did in my heart. I never told anyone in the family about it, I knew they would not understand it. It took me years to get over Dad's death. Maryann and I, with friends, would go out drinking on weekends and after a few beers I would speak about him and get emotional. I always felt no one understood my pain or knew what I was going through in my heart. I never felt heard. I was always the kid that did the right thing, trying my hardest to keep the peace, I was there but wasn't really there, I was dismissed because of it. I never really felt as though I had a voice in the family.

After Dad's death we faced other tragedies as a family. Suicide attempts. Deaths. Abuse. We faced these events without the help of faith. How we survived and stayed together is a miracle in itself. We just had to survive and get on with life and hope that just around the corner things would surprise us and show us there was more to life than what we were experiencing. But deep down I knew I was a sinner and I wondered if God was punishing us for that. I was still taking responsibility for everything.

Along with alcohol I looked for love in all the wrong places, and from the age of sixteen I was also smoking dope to relax me and help me to sleep. I once told my doctor about this and he said it was okay if it helped me, and as long as it was in small quantities. I was soon smoking dope regularly, but always after work because I understood the responsibility to hold down a job and work hard. I never believed in being high at work. I worked with children and would never place them at risk. The dope was a coping mechanism, I never really learnt to process pain, there was too much of it and it was a constant in my life. I wasn't a victim, I was a survivor: you get knocked down and you get up again. The knocks over the years took an unseen toll on my heart. The dope helped me to escape to a place of peace, a place where the burdens of life were lifted for a short time. I liked to be high, I liked it a lot. Mum didn't discover any of this until years later.

It is in the times of trauma that you question the purpose of life. I never found any answers. During my teenage years I didn't feel that I belonged anywhere. I didn't fit in at school and I didn't want to be at home because I felt unsafe there. Looking back, I'm amazed I lived a level of functionality in life, with housing, a good job, education, finance and a social group. People in our social group wanted to have a life like mine. I was doing well on a superficial level. Beneath the surface, however, was the ongoing experiences of dysfunction and the suppressed pain of years of unresolved issues. I didn't know how to process pain. I didn't know you were meant to. I never really knew or understood my worth and value and always considered other people's needs to be more important than my own. I felt that even as a child, and it carried into my teen years and adulthood.

It was a long time before I knew God's hand - His grace - on my life, but I believe that He heard that little seven-year-old's cry ...... on her knees beside her bed, crying out for help. I can see that picture in my mind so clearly today as if it was only a short time ago. Today I sense the smile of a loving father, loving that level of vulnerability and transparency. I believe that the only explanation for my ability to keep going was that God's spirit gave me courage to stand when I didn't think I could. Today I believe that He worked miracle after miracle for me; giving me the supernatural ability to get up again and fight for freedom, the right to a happy and a healthy future was on His agenda. I didn't know that at the time, but it is the only thing that makes sense today.

The most stabilising influence I had ever known came into my life when I was twenty-one. I met a man at the gym in the spa. I had just finished doing a workout with my best friend and Marko and his cousin (my best friend's boyfriend) were in the tub. He was attracted to me, it was obvious, but I initially said no. It didn't take long though and he won my heart. Not long after dating Marko, only a couple of months later, we knew it was serious. Our relationship was intimate and beautiful. He needed accommodation and so did I, plus Maryann and another friend, so we decided we would pool resources and rent a house together. Marko's love for me was genuine and I felt so loved, protected and supported. He stood with me as the disfunction continued to grow in my family; it brought us closer. He was a special man and a gift for the next season of my life.

After eight years together we decided to marry. The desire of my heart was to be a wife and a mum; we planned to create our own family and have a child, so we thought we should do it properly and get married. I wanted us to all have the same name - I was ready to see the dream that lived in my heart as a child become real. To become a mummy and a wife. Initially, we made plans for a huge church wedding and I asked Maryann to be Maid of honour and my best friends to be bridesmaids. They were so excited! Together we began to plan a very large traditional wedding. The plan for the bridal party was; four girls, and four boys and the venue was to be a large church in Adelaide. Everyone in our sphere was elated, we were seen as 'the match made in heaven.' Most of the people we knew wanted what we had, a life partner. I brought a beautiful traditional wedding dress, with an extremely long veil. It was stunning, a dress that all little girls dream about. I looked amazing in it and I was excited.

Marko and I were discussing wedding plans and I felt to ask him if he could make the choice about our wedding plans what would they be? He joked that elopement would his choice because it would be simpler, and cost less. We laughed about it and then we became more serious and as we discussed it further, we decided it was actually a good idea. So right then and there we changed our plans and decided on an elopement to Tasmania. I reorganised everything and apologised to the bridal party. We also planned to have a celebration with family and close friends when we returned home. We were happy with our new decision and knew that it was the right decision for us.

A few weeks before my fairytale wedding, eloping with my fiancé, I was really surprised to find that I was having doubts about the marriage. I talked to a close friend and we put it down to wedding jitters, so I dismissed the feelings. I continued to question my thoughts and reason with myself 'Hadn't I always wanted to get married and have a family, and be with Marko whom I loved deeply?' I never told Marko of these doubts and we were married on a beautiful day in January by a country river, Mountain River in Tasmania. I was dressed as a bride, Marko wore a tuxedo, and his Tasmanian friends witnessed the ceremony that was conducted by a celebrant. It was a beautiful day, a wedding that little girls dream of, an experience that was adventurous and romantic. A story that you would see in the movies. Our happiness was to be short lived.

Not long into our marriage there, was a string of tragic events in the family, all of them involving a death. Death scared the living daylights out of me because I had never fully recovered from my Dad's death.

However, we were overjoyed when I became pregnant. This was a baby so desperately wanted. We had endured eighteen months of fertility treatment. Each month there was the agony of a negative response and the torment of fear and doubt as we began yet another round of tablets to stimulate the reproduction cycle. I remember doing a head stand in my bed after an intimate moment, hoping that the egg would fertilise! Then came the elation as I learned of the results of the routine blood tests. I could hardly believe it. I was at work and did the routine call and rang the nurse for my results; a recent routine blood test that had been done a few days before. She said: 'Angie it's positive. Congratulations. You're pregnant.' I had to ask the nurse to check the results and repeat back to me that I was pregnant. It was like the feeling at Christmas when you open your present and you go in to shock, because it feels like you waited forever for it and then it was there; it was yours. I was going to be a mum, an incredible joy over took my heart, it was one of the happiest moments and memory in my life. I was finally going to fulfil what I believed was my life's purpose, I'm going to be a mummy. Marko was just as excited. We went together for the first scan at six weeks and held hands as we viewed our little one. The gynaecologist assured us that everything was fine.

In our excitement we told the people in our world, we were so proud. Our circle of family and friends shared out joy and were really excited for us. They knew the heartache we had endured to achieve this success. We prepared for our future as a family, and thought about names. I would rub my tummy and we giggled together as we talked to our little one. At the back of my mind I was aware that things sometimes go wrong, but I chose to concentrate on the joy and be positive.

Late one night I went to the toilet and experienced what felt like a knockout punch. I knew something was horribly wrong. No. No. No! This can't be happening. There was a cry from the deepest part of me. I still have memory of the cry that I let out. It spoke of a broken-ness that was beyond words, a grief without hope. The next twenty-four hours were a blur. The numbness was my body's way of coping with the shock. What had I done that was so bad; what had I done to deserve this? How could God let this happen? The cry of my heart was 'Why,

why?' My thoughts were like peak hour traffic at a major intersection. Why is there so much pain in my life? Is God punishing me? Had I been a bad person in my last life? Why is there so much suffering in the world? What's the purpose of it? Is there really a God?

Long ago I decided I didn't want to believe in God anymore. My Catholic upbringing convinced me that He was hard and judgmental, and I couldn't possibly believe in Him because He would punish me, for sure. I did believe in His existence because I believed that I must have offended Him; believing that is that's why I had faced constant trauma in my life. My conscious mind fought with my subconscious, trying to rationalise emotions I was incapable of processing. Emotionally raw, I came under a weight of grief that no words could articulate.

Maryann was with me when I had my first panic attack. I couldn't breathe, my mind went into overload, I could not think one rational thought. I was terrified. I wanted to run, but I couldn't move. I wanted to die. I pleaded with her to help me. She gave me a mild sleeping tablet and immediately made a doctor's appointment. My doctor prescribed the sedative, Seropax. I wasn't keen on taking medication but I was so fearful of another attack. I knew in my mind that I needed to do whatever it took to never experience an attack like that again. If it meant taking the drug to stop it, I decided that is what I needed to do. The doctor said that I needed time to process the loss, and he reassured me that if I were not stable in a week or so, he would refer me to a psychologist for counselling. I had no idea I was slipping into a depressive state. Marko was devastated. We grieved together. That week I lay on a mattress on the floor in the lounge room, with my faithful little Pomeranian, Molly, beside me. She was my comfort and she knew something was seriously wrong. I think she sensed my pain. I didn't have much to give, but she remained close. That week with suicidal thoughts trying to ambush me, I seriously, for the first time in my life, questioned whether I should make a plan and take my life. I decided that I couldn't do that to Marko.

Marko was patient with me and allowed me the time I needed to grieve. I never told him my suicidal thoughts because I didn't want to scare him. To be honest, I was terrified about them myself. I knew my dad's history and I never wanted to be like him. About a week later Marko came home from work. It was during that day that I had made a decision to get up from the knock-out punch and move forward with life. As Marko walked in the door, I said 'Babe, do you want to go down the beach tonight.' The beach always brought peace and cleared my mind. If I needed perspective, it was the place I visited. Life seems to make sense at the beach to me and being there has the ability to bring clarity and healthy perspective. Marko was overjoyed! Without communicating it to me, I knew he understood that I had taken a big step forward. It was time to reconnect with life and to our future. Molly also loved the beach so we took her with us and headed down to Semaphore beach. We walked for miles and talked as we walked hand in hand, Molly beside us. Molly was like our baby, she was even fed by a spoon at times, a spoilt little princess. She did most things with us, she was an important part of our life.

Marko, Molly and I walked back to the car; Molly close to us. Then from seemingly nowhere, while we were in the car park, a car hit Molly. Molly cried out, loudly. Marko ran to her, held her tight and she died in his arms. The trauma of witnessing such an event took me to the edge. It took Marko there also. A lady came and gave us a sheet as hysteria was all around us. The beach was crowded that day. The lady that hit Molly was apologising profusely. In my world, everything was in slow motion, and had no sound. My heart was screaming: "This cannot be happening. This is just a bad dream. A nightmare." Marko took charge of the situation and placed Molly in the back seat of thecar. I stood on the curb and vomited violently. We drove home in complete silence with our hearts trying to process what had just happened. It's an understatement to say that I was an emotional mess. We both needed support so when we got home, we called family. Maryann was there in what seemed like seconds and called Marko's brother so that he could support Marko. Marko went outside and started digging a hole, but was devastated and was struggling to do what he needed to do. Together, Marko and his brother buried our little friend. Marko called me over so that I could say goodbye; I stood at the grave, numb and suffering in deep, deep pain; grief that I hope that you never have to experience. I believe now that we were living under a curse and it inflicted so much pain. Trauma after trauma followed us.

....

My friend Karen came to comfort me when she heard about the miscarriage and Molly's death. Karen was into alternative therapies. When she heard that I had been prescribed Seropax for panic attacks she strongly urged me to see a naturopath and insisted on paying the initial fee.

My first visit to the naturopath was in mid 2000. I was introduced to her by Karen. The naturopath was a skinny lady, I knew she was an 'alternative type' by the way she dressed, she was really pale, softly spoken and she had long wavy reddish hair, tied back. She would have been in her early to mid-forties. On the first visit she explained that I couldn't combine natural remedies with prescribed medications. She asked me to make a choice about the treatment I wanted to receive, either the Seropax that was prescribed by the doctor or the natural remedies. I agreed to give the natural remedies a try. I was a bit dubious and nervous of her at first. I hoped she wouldn't ask too many questions because I wasn't confident I would be able to keep my emotions together. I was scared of having a panic attack in front of her. She handed me a small glass containing a liquid herbal mixture. I remember the consulting room had a strange smell. It smelt a little like the drink that she handed me. I was told to drink the mixture slowly and to keep it under my tongue. She asked me to take off my shoes and then gestured for me to sit in a comfortable chair. She then commenced reflexology on my feet which, together with the herbs and to my amazement, made me feel incredibly relaxed. She asked me about childhood illnesses and the recent events that had led me to her office. I was so relaxed that I talked to her without any anxiety for an hour. She prescribed particular herbs for depression and emergency drops for anxiety and panic attacks. She reassured me that she was confident she could help me with my infertility problems, too, once I was emotionally stable and strong again. She said 'give me six months, and you will be ready to try for a baby again.' She was a great listener and showed genuine empathy. I sensed she was moved by my story. There was a definite connection between us.

A week later I made another appointment because I was still struggling with depression and anxiety and I thought that my drops needed to be increased. Again, she was so compassionate and caring. I thought to myself, this lady is so sensitive; she holds wisdom. She had a gift to be able to comfort me and offer a helpful perspective: different ways of looking at or thinking about situations that troubled me. Never before had I experienced any type of counsel like this. I was impressed with the spiritual nature of her counselling. I didn't know what it was, I just knew she cared and that she was committed to helping me. She was warm, she expressed love and hope in a truly difficult time I was thankful that I had met her, and was also thankful that I made the choice - to take the path of natural medicine.

During one appointment we were talking about the loss of my baby. I was fearful because I didn't know where my baby was and her explanation was that she believed that the souls of some deceased people sometimes get 'stuck'. She believed that women have miscarriages so that the souls of deceased people can 'move on to the other side'. It sounded like a reasonable explanation at the time. I accepted this perspective because it seemed to me that it offered something positive from the trauma. Maybe my baby died so that someone could live? it took the sting out of the grief when I accepted that as truth. Deep down I knew it wasn't truth... I just wanted it to be. They mystery of her spiritual philosophy intrigued me. I was looking for answers to all my big questions. I asked question after question, baring my heart on an extremely deep level with her. She always had an answer and they were always different to what I was expecting. Radically different! They were perspectives that I had never heard before. They made me question life in a new way and I liked the mystery of it. There were no limits, no wright, no wrong... the philosophy had its own answers, no accountability, just free thought. At the time I was incredibly vulnerable, I began to allow her into my heart and enjoyed the 'feel good' sense of connection I had with her. Her philosophies became more and more appealing. She seemed so wise and I knew she was a lady who had asked a lot of the deep questions in life and I was needing deep life perspectives. In my opinion, she had good answers to my probing questions. I responded well to both her counselling and her remedies and in a couple of months I was stable. What I didn't understand was that her New Age spirituality was closely connected to the occult. The counsel she provided was steeped in witchcraft and occult practice. She practised witchcraft and was unaware of the spiritual connections that she was making. I don't see her as evil and she wasn't a bad person, she was actually trying to help. She was a white witch, but her intentions were good.

TWO

INTO THE OCCULT

I wanted to connect with truth and I wanted wisdom like my naturopath. My understanding was that she had attained a place of spiritual enlightenment and she had good answers to life because of her own spiritual journey. I wanted that. I wanted to share in the same experiences, so I took her spiritual beliefs on board and accepted them as my own. It was the greatest mistake of my life.

If I can give you any advice through my personal life experience, please let it be this: individuals do not have all the answers, especially not to the questions I was asking. My naturopath counselled me from her own place of pain and confusion. She too had issues with the Catholic church, the Catholic God and she also rejected the teachings of the church. What I didn't understand at the time was that she created her own personal spiritual philosophy based on bad experiences. I know now that this is very dangerous and can open spiritual doors that are not meant to be opened. I identified with her past and this formed the basis for my connection with her. I believed that she understood me. In the spirit we both knew that the Catholic God was not what we believed, that decision was ok, but it wasn't ok to make up our own personal philosophy so that we could feel better about life. That's what the New Age does. It creates its own humanistic philosophy based on life experience, on feelings. It's not a good idea. I gave my naturopath so much trust, accepting her and allowing her into an influential role in my life but taking on her belief systems I unknowingly placed myself at extreme risk. I lost my personal identity, what I believed, what life had taught me and became dependent on hers. I relinquished personal morals and values and all sense of individual empowerment. The reality of New Age practice is that it is in opposition to absolutes.

The official start of my journey into the occult began many months after meeting my naturopath. During one session I told her that I thought I had some psychic ability and described my experiences with tarot cards. My mum's nephew had read my cards one night when they were visiting. Mum was there and we all had ours cards read. I would have been about eight years of age. We all thought that it was harmless fun. Years earlier I also had one session with a clairvoyant. I had not become seriously involved in these experiences with alternative spiritual modalities, but I was always looking to connect with the spiritual in me. As a young child I had a 'knowing' that spiritual truth was missing in my life, and because of it I never felt whole. I was determined to find that missing piece of the puzzle. My naturopath asked if my psychic ability was more suited to these three occult practices - tarot, clairvoyance or Reiki. I exclaimed 'Reiki', having recently read a book about it and been intrigued by the concept, of inner healing and the principles of Reiki which was hands-on healing with an emphasis on love, light and inner healing. My naturopath gave me the name and phone number of a Reiki practitioner. 'You will love her,' she said.

I enrolled to do Reiki 1 with a Reiki master I will refer to as Amanda. Far from loving her, I felt uneasy from the first meeting. Everything in me screaming that something wasn't right, my belly felt uneasy... unfortunately I chose to ignore it. I should have listened. It proved to be another difficult life lesson learnt the hard way.

Amanda began with the history of Reiki and explained that it was to do with 'energies'. We were led by Amanda to invite the energy into us by closing our eyes and visualising walking along a path into a temple. Before we began she burnt something and waved it around us and told us it was to clear away any negative energy. Then we lit candles. When Amanda made symbols over us with her hands I was immediately overcome by extreme heat. I understood this to be the power of Reiki and I felt excited. The uneasiness I had felt previously, vanished. I believed I had received healing hands; I had received the power to heal people. New Age practices are all about personal power, encouraging egotism and a god complex. They believe that the power is from within you. It is first received from an external source, however from that point, the power is from you. I was encouraged to practise healing people as much as possible and I became an advocate for Reiki, laying hands on anyone who would let me. My hands became very hot, heat emanated from me and into those that I placed my hands on. Together we understood in no uncertain terms that I had the power. I decided that I wanted to become a Reiki master myself, attaining to the highest level and teaching it to others. I thought I was on my path to supernatural enlightenment and success. Believing I was now mentally and emotionally stable, I was elated at the prospect of discovering all the answers to the questions that bothered me, attaining true spiritual enlightenment and ultimate healing.

Amanda also encouraged me to meditate regularly; to connect with the spiritual realm. I trusted her advice because she had been a Reiki teacher for fifteen years - she had also abandoned Christianity. I borrowed a book that explained how to get into a meditative state and embraced everything that I read. I was a woman on a mission. I set out to read many New Age books and absorbing and applying each of the principles as my own. A lot of the books that I read were in the local public library, the same library where I borrowed the Reiki book. The cry of my heart was to find that missing puzzle piece and live in a place of forgiveness, love, light and healing. That feeling that I felt as a child; of needing to find that connection was still in my soul.

I meditated alone every night. On a mattress on the lounge room floor, with my candle, and all other lights turned off in the house, I would go through my ritual of centering and grounding and emptying myself and my mind. Then I would lie down, relax and try to connect with the spiritual realm. After several weeks I was able to imagine white light. I was starting to connect with something out there. I was detaching from myself, from the world. There was a peace and an excitement attached to these sessions.

After much practice and many months of research, suppressed childhood memories began to surface during these sessions and I started to see colours – orange, red, yellow, green, blue - very clear and bright. I assumed that I was connecting more spiritually and the colours that I was seeing was a part of my healing gift. With Amanda's ongoing encouragement I read and researched, learning more about New Age concepts and practice, incorporating all of it into my own belief system, and lifestyle. Along with continued sessions with my naturopath, I studied chakras, went to yoga, developed a physical six-pack on my stomach, cleansed my physical system, and was encouraged by the improvement in my mood and health. I was living on a high. The positive emotions and experiences reinforced my conviction that I was on my way to spiritual enlightenment. I confidently preached New Age concepts to anyone who would listen. Marko was supportive during this whole process. He always supported me and just wanted to see me happy. He was my greatest encourager.

Many of the books I read talked about visions during meditation and the supernatural reality of connecting with all sorts of characters and creatures.

I was now entering the meditative state with ease and was soon seeing visions of angels, doves and white light. These visions initially were pleasant, calm, and encouraging. I began levitating. I would feel myself leaving the floor, and sometimes my body. I was going deeper and deeper, emptying my mind and opening myself to the spiritual realm. There were times when I felt myself entering into a spiritual space and would get fearful and pull myself out of it. Eventually I learnt to go with it and enjoy the experience. I even saw what I thought was Jesus, but it was only a character in white.

I wanted to go to a deeper level of spiritual healing and it was recommended by Amanda that I see Cindy, who lived in the Barossa Valley. I told Cindy about my childhood experiences. I really wanted to let them go and be healed. Cindy explained that the physical body stores negative energy that results from negative experiences and mindsets. She assured me she could remove those things from my body using crystals and essences. I lay down on a massage bed and she moved around me, apparently cleansing my aura and the negative energy within. I had many sessions with her, always starting with a counselling time which exposed the negative energy to enabled its removal. In these sessions I relived the trauma of emotional, mental, physical and sexual abuse experiences. My whole past was in my head and it was overwhelming.

During meditation I wrote down all the things I felt guilty about and wanted to let go of, and then I burnt the notes. I did this constantly, writing things I regretted. The idea was to give them to the universe. I revisited my childhood where there was so much pain that had never been addressed. I recall looking at a professionally drawn portrait of myself as a child. There was so much pain in her eyes. I took the drawing outside and burnt it. It was during this time that I truly decided there was no God and committed myself to deeper levels of New Age philosophy.

My focus was now on the universe, divine cosmos and karma. Karma is the belief that we have many lives and we keep coming back until we learn the lessons properly and get it right. I was determined to get it right in this life because I didn't want to come back again. Many people explore their past lives while in a meditative state, but I didn't want to. I had a strong sense of guilt about mine. I thought I had been a murderer, and that this was why I had suffered so much in this life. What a deception this was and how heavy a burden it added to the pain I carried from my childhood.

Courage Over Adversity

A couple of months after doing Reiki 1; I agreed to do Reiki 2. I expected it to be just more heat and more healing ability. I had no idea what it was really about and I didn't ask.

ANGIE AMUSO

THE MAD MOUSE RIDE OF MY LIFE

I nervously buy my ticket for the mad mouse ride
My stomach churns as I click into my seat belt, adrenaline pumping
I have tingles covering every inch of my insides and outsides.
I'm really not that confident, I feel vulnerable, but it's too late NOW!
I tell myself, 'Hey Kiddo, hang tight, deep breaths, cope the best you know how'.
For this huge monstrosity was always much fear, had such a hold on me,
I knew I needed to face it head on, not run, the time is meant to be.
Off I go, the car wobbles faster and shakes, oh! what have I done?
I think to myself, 'Hey, this is no fun'.
A sudden body-slamming turn to the right,
I scream, but no voice is heard, my mind is crazy, I can't see an end in sight.

Courage Over Adversity

My internals have no time to recover, ever so quickly from left to right,
I feel I will slip from this mingy belt that holds me in,
Subconsciously knowing my grip will keep me alright.
My fingers are red, my knuckles turn white, I clutch the bar so damn tight.
A speeding thunderbolt, I descend on a fifty-degree angle, 'round and 'round we go.
Why did I take the risk, I want to know?
At this moment I feel a mess, my fears putting me to the test.
People below oblivious to my stress, casually walk around,
Looking like little ants on the ground.
The sharp corners, these turns, this machine moving at rapid pace
The hurling gushing wind blowing in my face.
Mad machine slows down, mind stops racing, body calms, the end is near.
I think, 'Yes I did it, I faced this fear.'
Mad machine comes to a halt
Electric energy gives me a jolt
Not really so bad, after all?
My ghostly face and ungrounded body slide so slowly down the wall.

Reiki 2 was more intense, with many symbols to be learned. Similar to Reiki 1, we started with a visualisation in a meditative state, during which I saw a vision of my Nan. She looked very upset. During the ritual to take us into the next level one of my fellow students saw a dagger and heard an audible voice telling her she was going to die. Amanda interpreted this as meaning the old life was making way for the new, and made reference to the death card in tarot. I was concerned, especially as it came after my dark vision of Nan. I felt uneasy but Amanda was dismissive about them both. To my eyes, she seemed a little rattled when we shared these things with her; she tried to hide it, but I noticed.

In the afternoon we learnt about absent healing, where people get healed from a distance by calling in their energies and using the symbols. We were now getting into full-on rituals. I had no idea of the ramifications of such practices. During that same afternoon, Amanda spoke over me, telling me I was going to go on a different spiritual path, that I was going to follow Jesus. I listened to what she had to say but I didn't really believe it. I had entered into the realm of humanistic philosophy - in the New Age you apply absolutely anything that sounds good. A little bit of Jesus, a little bit of Buddha, you create your own belief system based on your own preferences. There are no boundaries, no guidelines, no safeguards. It was a rollercoaster ride into a spiritual sphere that brought me close to death. Reiki had taken me into witchcraft in a deep and intense way. I innocently fell into it.

That night I decided that if I was going to do absent healing on others I should practise on myself. I had heaps of excess baggage I hadn't dealt with. What I didn't realise at the time was that I was about to make a decision to enter into a ritual that would dangerously change the course of my life. I had no idea it would take me over the edge into a place of darkness, torment and insanity. I was about to experience hell on earth. If only I knew, I never would have made this decision.

I began by asking my subconscious and conscious to merge. I thought this would allow any unresolved issues in my subconscious to make their way to my conscious mind where I could deal with them and live in the inner healing I so desperately sought. How unexperienced and unaware I was. I innocently used the symbols I had learnt that day and followed every step I had been taught. I heard a loud bang in my space and something forced its way into my world. Uninvited, it just launched itself into this place, close to me, and from that point on an audible voice entered my spiritual space. At first this voice spoke direction and words of comfort. It spoke politely. It continued in this manner for several weeks. I felt uneasy about it because my dad had a history with voices and I didn't like it there. The only problem was I didn't know how to get rid of it. I asked it to leave and it wouldn't. As I went deeper into this level of spiritual enlightenment the visions got darker and the voice became loud, angry and abusive.

I began seeing visions of skulls and crosses, and stained glass shattering, and the voice swore profanities and screamed at me to harm myself. It became more and more aggressive until it was abusing not only me but those I loved and those that were the closest to me. This thing was trying to take over my mind and I was scared. The next stage of abuse was actual physical assault. I began to have violent seizures during meditation. My eyes would twitch and then roll back into my head so that I couldn't see. These episodes lasted five minutes at a time, and each one left me emotionally, mentally and physically exhausted. I was in a battle for my life.

Amanda and others I related to in New Age understood that I had got caught in a dark place in the spiritual realm. They reassured me that I had a problem of a spiritual nature and their advice was to increase my involvement in even more New Age concepts and practices. I did as I was directed. It wasn't a time to question. I needed a solution, and quickly. For many months I fought this thing in my own strength and understanding. The voices attacked me constantly, in an internal and external war. I dared not speak of it, not even to my immediate family. How could I explain it to them? I wanted to protect them, not create fear. I bought more crystals and essences for protection, and did the clearing and cleaning rituals that were associated with each one. My focus was all on protection as fear entered my heart and soul, and I searched for the way out of the mess I had got myself into.

Then I met a lady in one of the Reiki groups who told me she knew a Muslim leader who could help me. At a meeting in his office I explained my spiritual issues to him, and he said, 'You have a demon and it needs to come out. I can deliver you.' He asked me to lie on a hard bed that was in the corner of his office and then he prayed a prayer over me, expecting the demon to go. It didn't. He explained that I would need to become a Muslim for it to leave. I agreed. I was so desperate for freedom I would do anything. He was pleased and gave me a book that explained the Muslim faith. He explained that demons live in pictures and told me to take down any photos that I had in my house that showed a person or animal. So I went home and took down all our wedding photos and anything that had animals in it.

The Muslim book he gave me told me about the things I should do, how I was to pray, what I could and couldn't do. I couldn't eat bacon and I had to pray many times a day, in a very specific way. It was difficult. My mum knew something was wrong when I took down all my wedding photos. I told her she needed to trust me and that I had met a man who told me what was important for me to do. I confessed Allah as God and that he was the only God, but the reality was it was just a sentence the book told me to say - it wasn't something I actually believed. A few weeks later I decided I couldn't live in the Muslim faith. It didn't seem like the right path. I walked away from the Muslim faith and I never saw that man again.

....

My Dad was a diagnosed schizophrenic and as children were told it could be genetically passed on to us. We understood he was a tormented man and we didn't want to be like him. Sometimes what we most fear is what comes upon us. Fearing what doctors might tell me, I did everything I could to avoid medical intervention. I knew the label they would place on my life.

I tried desperately to find a solution. Months went by, with me applying one new age concept after another to resolve the problem, but then one night the voice gave me a choice. It screamed: 'You or your family!' It meant, either I or my family must die, and insisted I decide which. There are no words to describe this level of spiritual oppression. For eight months this thing tried to kill me. The pressure to make a decision brought on even more severe seizures. My weight dropped to an unhealthy level and I was losing the battle for my mind. I was tormented to physical and psychological exhaustion. I could not let my family suffer because of the choices I had made. I had to protect them. It was time. I knew what I had to do.

My husband was in bed, my best friend was sleeping in the lounge, so I went into the spare room and took some marijuana for courage. The voice was intense, like a megaphone screaming in my ear, counting down, giving me orders about my death sentence. The marijuana was a mistake because it sent me into a trance, but I'd made the decision and I had to follow through. I was exhausted, with no solution to the problem I had been fighting for over six months. I took a kitchen knife into the shower cubicle. I hurt myself badly and waited to fall into unconsciousness. But I didn't. I willed myself into unconsciousness, longed for death, and still nothing happened. I sat on the floor and wondered who to wake up to drive me to hospital. I could not tell Marko what I had just done. I couldn't face the hurt in his eyes. I woke my friend and she wanted to tell Marko but I begged her not to. By now the pain was excruciating and I was in and out of reality. I had finally stepped over the line of insanity and I knew it.

At the hospital the voice was trying to take over my mind and I remember repeating 'My name is Angie Amuso, my name is Angie Amuso'. I was trying desperately to hold onto my identity. It is difficult to express my sorrow at what I had put my family and friends through. I had tried so hard to come through without worrying or hurting them. I thought I was doing them a favour by choosing my death instead of theirs. I was so frightened of hurting them that I begged the doctors to put me in a straightjacket, but the nurses gave my friend a blanket and she tied it around me instead, to help me feel more secure. Two female psychiatrists came from the mental health team to assess me. I told them I needed to be locked up, but they wanted to put me in an open ward in the psychiatric unit. I was so fearful the voice would make me hurt someone else and I begged them to lock me up. I remember both women crying, moved by my grief and fear. They were gentle and did their best to reassure me.

I was taken by ambulance to Glenside Hospital, lock up facility. It was like a prison. All the way I kept saying my name over and over. I thought I would spend the rest of my life incarcerated in that mental institution. The voice said I would, and I believed it. I remember little of the following week. The doctors explained to my family that my mind had reached overload and it had to be shut down medically to give it rest. When I was fully conscious again I saw I was in a prison. There were bars in the small enclosed outdoor area and heavily locked doors on the inside. There was no escaping, not that I thought about that. I wasn't disruptive, unlike some others who had to be forcibly restrained by five to six staff members and medicated by injection. I wanted to do everything I could to sort myself out. I knew I needed help and I wasn't going to fight it.

A week later I was transferred to an open psychiatric ward closer to home. I weighed little more than

35 kg yet I was on twice the normal adult dose of medication for seizures, depression, anxiety and the voices. The medications caused severe reactions where my legs shook constantly. It's called restless legs. It was torture to not be able to relax. They changed my medications and instantly my legs no longer shook.

THREE

SALVATION

My loved ones feared that I was dying on the inside, and they were looking for answers. When a family friend named Dawn enquired after me, Maryann explained the spiritual search I had been on and that the doctors had diagnosed schizo-effective disorder which, in their opinion was an illness I would have for the rest of my life. Dawn realised there was a desperate need for spiritual intervention. She had recently become a follower of Jesus and she knew He was the answer. She visited me and assured me her church fellowship was praying for me. I was open to all the support I could get.

Dawn continued to visit, encouraging me and listening to my story as I tried to explain what was happening to me. She showed a loving concern for me and spoke respectfully about God and Jesus.

Eventually, I told her I wasn't interested in Christianity but I respected her beliefs. In my mind I associated God with the Catholic church and that God scared me. I knew she was trying to help me though, and I was grateful. On one occasion she visited on a day when I was in a high state of anxiety, experiencing panic attacks and insisting I be returned to the hospital. Dawn calmed me and asked if her pastors could visit me.

The pastors, Peter and Sallyanne, seemed genuinely interested in me and listened patiently as I shared my new age philosophies and recent experiences. When Peter spoke, he was gentle and shared the Christian message in a way that made sense to me. I was interested in what Peter and Sallyanne had to say, but the voice didn't like them at all. It abused them in my head, and tried to distract me during the conversation. I was constantly measuring the information they shared to see how it related to the New Age teaching. Finally, I exclaimed: 'I can believe everything you say, but I can't accept there is a devil.' Subconsciously I knew that if I believed in the devil's existence I would have to accept that it was the devil who was attacking me. This scared me. Peter didn't argue but respected my right to choose. He offered to pray for me and explained it would be more serious and spiritually dangerous if he prayed as if I were a Christian. He released a simple blessing over my life. I was grateful. I believe valuable seeds were sown at this time; seeds that were to produce a harvest in the future. Meanwhile, I was still practising new age rituals, desperately clutching at straws. Deep down I knew I was on the wrong road.

Dawn continued to visit me every day. I was having severe panic attacks and seizures, but she kept calm, listened, and talked about Jesus. It was interesting that she could speak about God as much as she liked, but the minute she spoke about Jesus the voice would get violent and scream in anger. I started to connect the attacks to the conversation. It was always the name of Jesus that provoked that thing to rage. Dawn's patience, her love and persistence, was amazing. I was hospitalised many times over the next six months and I appreciated that she continued to be there for me. She refused to give up.

The hospital kept changing my medications, trying different drugs and dosages, but nothing seemed to help, which reinforced in my mind that the issues were spiritual more than medical. Every time I talked to the doctors about when the voice entered, the night of the ritual, I tried desperately to get them to understand that this was a spiritual issue. They detained me longer, increased the dosage of medication and placed a label on my condition. I was not in denial, but I refused that label: 'schizophrenia'. Eventually I learned to say nothing. I knew I would have to cooperate if I wanted a future outside of a mental institution. I recall one day whilst I was in hospital the main doctor said that they wanted to do an assessment on me, asking for my permission for several doctors to hear my story. I agreed and sat in the room with three doctors dressed in corporate suits. I shared honestly my experiences with Reiki and the ritual that I had done on myself and how the voice entered into my head at the moment. They looked at each other and my doctor said, 'so many people sit in that chair and tell us the same thing, exactly the same.' I was relieved to hear that, I thought, that's good... they didn't see it the same way, they increased my medication and kept me in hospital longer. They explained to me that in their professional opinion I was not ready for discharge. Everyone in my family had accepted what they feared, but I would not.

Dawn was the only person who agreed that it was a spiritual issue. I remember wishing there was a book, something documented in black and white that could give me the solution to my problem. Little did I know that there was such a book. There was an opposition doing its best to keep me from that truth. But Dawn refused to give up on me. One day we were sitting on the lawns in front of the mental hospital and I asked, 'What's that prayer about, you know, the "our father" one?' She showed me where it was in scripture and gave me some insight as to its meaning. I laid back on the grass, raised my arms to the sky and said, 'Okay, if You are real, will You show me?' That was an important moment because I opened myself to the possibility of the truth...the spiritual truth that I had always searched for. I still had some way to journey and it would take time.

There was still a strong pull to stay in New Age, but none of the people I was connected to there could help me. I had exhausted their understanding and resources. I believe that caused them to fear. I tried to maintain contact, but they never visited me in hospital and eventually the relationships ended. I continued to apply new age remedies in vain and I wasn't responding to medication, either. Someone had to be with me all the time because I was constantly battling the war in my head. The voice was internal and external; sometimes speaking inside and then yelling at me from a distance. It could change its sound from male to female and it spoke vile profanities night and day. I was still having seizures and, once again, losing the will to live. I was exhausted. The doctors predicted I would eventually suicide. Medical science is limited in what it can do.

I went home on a short break from hospital and Dawn was with me. She was sharing about Jesus as usual, and this time the inner voice went berserk. I never knew what its limitations were, what powers it had, how far it could go. I didn't know if it could do what it said it could so I was worried for Dawn's safety. Dawn continued speaking about Jesus and the thing in my head screamed. I realised its extreme reaction to the name of Jesus indicted His power. It was time. I decided to give my life to Jesus.

....

Dawn rang her home group leader and arranged for me to make my decision official at the small group meeting that same night. In the hours leading up to the meeting I experienced many violent seizures and intense attacks from the voice, but I was determined to follow through with the decision I had made to be there.

As I was being introduced to Bazz, the leader, I started to have a seizure. Bazz placed his hand on my shoulder and said, 'In the name of Jesus I command you to stop.' And I stopped shaking. I was amazed. I'd had at least fifteen seizures already that day, I need to know what was it was about Bazz that made this one stop? I needed what he had. I was asked to sit down next to Bazz. When a few moments later I had another seizure, he did the same thing, calmly commanding it to stop in the name of Jesus. It never occurred to me to wonder what the other people in the room might be thinking about all of this, and no one panicked. Somehow, this confirmed to me that I'd made the right decision to be there.

Bazz went on to explain that Jesus holds all authority and this thing had to submit to that. He said it was like a police officer having authority over traffic; when he says stop, the traffic must obey and submit to his authority. Bazz led me in a prayer where I invited Jesus into my heart and life. I asked for forgiveness and asked Him to lead my life. I had a vision of Jesus – truly Jesus, not something that pretended to be him – and felt a release in my head. Something was different. There was joy in my heart.

The people in the group were friendly, and inquisitive, and over coffee I was able to speak freely about parts of my journey. I was accepted, not judged, and I felt comfortable and relaxed. I realised that I needed to build a relationship with Jesus in reading His word, in prayer and fellowship with others, and by trusting Him. Gradually, I handed over my weakness to Christ, allowing Him to strengthen me, but the battle for my soul was not over.

My grace is sufficient for you, for my power is made perfect in weakness ~ 2 Corinthians 12:9

Dawn visited and she had something to discuss. Confronting me gently, she explained the importance for me to sever all connections with the New Age movement, and with anything that related to its beliefs and practices. I was at a crossroad. If I was serious about following Jesus it was important that I let go of the New Age idols and practices I had held in my life. Dawn was honest, gracious and empathised, understanding that New Age was entrenched in my life at every level. There was a lot of stuff that had to go. Together we went through my house and filled several garbage bags with the crystals, books, essences, incense, necklaces and ornaments that I had collected. It was difficult getting rid of those things, there was a constant, daily pull I felt to go back into the New Age. Dawn walked the journey with me and disposed of the bags for me in a large dumpster in the community; some distance away where I couldn't get it back.

I came under severe attack every time I prayed or read the Bible, but I persevered. I was determined to build a relationship with Jesus no matter what the cost. I tried to hold all thoughts captive, always separating myself from the voice, thinking of it as an external influence and refusing to accept it as my own thoughts. This was a key to my ultimate victory and without this strategy I don't think I would have been set free. There was so much traffic in my head it was hard to concentrate or even converse with people. There was no escape, even during sleep. I was still highly medicated and still having many seizures and episodes where my eyes rolled back in my head. After six months as a Christian I was again emotionally, mentally and physically exhausted. I had fought for freedom, but the battle was not yet over. I had tried so hard to stand in the truth, but now I feared I had exhausted all options.

Listening to the bombardment of lies every day took its toll. The constant that was screamed at me was that even God had given up on me. This daily attack that I would hear began to feel real. After many weeks I decided that God had rejected me, I was still facing hell head on, with daily accusations, threats, and profanity and I seriously couldn't see a way out of the mess that I had got myself into. The situation seemed worse...... in fact, life became even more difficult when I invited Jesus into my life. Feeling as though I was doing everyone a favour, I attempted suicide for the second time. It was not an easy decision to come to. I put in weeks of planning, considering the ramifications. It takes a lot of courage to attempt to take your life. The pain became unbearable, and I couldn't live this hell forever. Deciding it was time, I took a very large overdose of my medication. I had planned it carefully waiting for the right time. I wrote brief a goodbye letter, and left it beside me. All too conscious of the pressure my family was under, I felt as though I was a burden. People judge mental health issues harshly and I felt a lot of shame attached to my situation. I felt even more shame because now I was a Christian.

I went to my bedroom and laid down and peacefully fell asleep. This was all that I remember while awake. While I was unconscious from the overdose, I heard a voice, not the usual angry one, but a voice that spoke with calm authority. It told me, 'You have two choices, the long road or the short road.' Immediately I heard my heart say 'loooong road.' somehow I had made a decision for the long road. Not long after I woke up with Mum and Maryann by my side, they were shocked when I woke because the doctors had just explained to them that I was slipping deeper into unconsciousness and the prognosis wasn't promising. Medical science believed that I was about to die. They sat by my side believing I was going to pass away. God had better plans, and I awoke. It was a such a relief to them. When I awoke I clearly remembered the choice that I had made in the darkness for the long road. It seemed to me that God had spoken it for me, in the natural I had made my decision to permanently leave this life, I have no other idea why I heard the long road, it must have been God helping me make a good decision. I also questioned God about the darkness; I asked him why was it that all I saw was darkness? His response was ""You were hidden under the shadow of my hand.' I was holding you.

Today, I know how to draw on His strength, but back then I had come to the end of myself with no ability to endure. I felt ashamed that, as a Christian, I had tried to attempt suicide, but Peter and Sallyanne, the pastors of my church, were not judgmental. They visited me in the hospital, held my hand, comforted me with scripture and stood in the gap and prayed. Their love spoke of God's unconditional love. I thank God for their commitment to me, for just being there, for having faith that this mess would work out, that God had a plan and purpose for my life. They didn't preach at me, they just loved me.

My family decided I was not well enough to make decisions, and certainly not ones that involved being a Christian. They banned all contact with the people from church and I wasn't allowed to attend meetings until they were convinced I was in a healthy mental state to make informed decisions. Everything I said and did was documented and I had no legal rights. There were endless discussions about me with the doctors and if I had day leave from hospital, I was never left alone. These restrictions only reinforced my fears that I was a risk to society and myself. I withdrew even more. This was so different to the highly independent woman I had been.

It was to be a long journey back to health and freedom but many people prayed for me during this time. Dawn had given me a book called Reduce me to Love, by Joyce Meyer. It sat on my bedside drawers in the hospital and though I didn't have much understanding of the Bible, I had this book. I have clear memories of lying in the mental hospital bed praying in the darkness while I was having violent seizures, and the cry that came from my heart was: 'Reduce me to love, reduce me to love.' God will you reduce me to love. Over and over, I would repeat it, and that became my constant prayer. I held onto that sentence and I cried out to heaven as often as I needed. The seizures continued in the darkness in that ward, but my prayer remained consistent; 'God, reduce me to love'. Behind closed doors the church reached out in love, always asking what they could do for me. Christian friends were not allowed to visit me, but they continued to pray and stand in the gap.

After many months I was allowed to make the decision to go back to church and continue on the path of following Jesus. I knew there was no other option and, reluctantly, my immediate family agreed. They continued to be suspicious of the church and to oppose my connection to it, but it was vital to my spiritual healing. Understanding Jesus and truth as well as my spiritual growth was my pathway to freedom. I knew that my future and ultimately, my life, depended on it. Ironically they were the words that the Reiki Master Amanda had spoken over me!

It was a significant day when I stood with a small group in church believing for my miracle, fighting in prayer for my freedom. At the altar of my church we stood in a circle, me in the centre. They prayed passionately, fighting with me and for me. Eventually Peter said: 'Angie, I want you to start claiming the truth, you need to take a stand.' Something rose up from my belly deep within me; and I yelled, 'Yes! Enough is ENOUGH! I have had enough of being pushed around by this bully in my head. No more!'

I'll never forget when I looked up and saw the smiles on their faces. It was time to know my authority in Christ and use it. I was surprised by what had come out of my mouth. For so long, I had been quiet, passive and very afraid, but something important changed in that moment. I had found some courage and it felt so good. From that moment on the attacks and the voice gradually decreased in intensity and frequency. But I still had seizures which limited my independence in many ways, including being able to drive. I explained this issue with a man that was consistent in his concern for me at church; weekly he would look for me and see how I was doing. He offered to pray for me with another man. I agreed and was taken to a private room for prayer specifically for the seizures to stop. While I was receiving prayer I immediately felt relaxed, then experienced a feeling of intense love and a beautiful presence came over me. I fell backwards. They caught me and gently laid me on the floor. I lay on the floor for quite a long time, experiencing the presence of the Holy Spirit for the very first time. As the presence increased I felt something leave my body. At that moment our prayers were answered and there were no more seizures. Another huge hurdle had been overcome.

My faithful friend, Dawn, continued to support me and I had weekly counselling appointments with Peter and Sallyanne. It was there that I dealt with the issues from my past experiences in the occult and the trauma of coming out of it. Many people in my life did not understand me - my family, people in the church, especially the medical staff that were caring for me. Pete and Sallyanne were trustworthy people, they stood with me in the 'crazy' and believed for my freedom. I could tell them anything. I maintained a very honest relationship with them and I appreciated their perspective, love and support. There was much healing and deliverance needed for the trauma that I experienced, like an onion being peeled layer after layer, releasing the agreements and traumatic experiences that I had been involved in. We worked through the issues slowly, one at a time. Those sessions were key to the freedom that I live in today. I also continued with prayer meetings and the home group. I did the new

Christian's course, 'Alpha', three times because assimilating information was still difficult for me. I was determined to do whatever was necessary for my freedom - another important key.

Water baptism was another significant milestone and after this many things started to turn around for the good for me. The baptism was postponed several times due to injuries I had in a recent car accident but finally the day arrived and I took that next step in obedience. I informed my family of my intention to be baptised, but because of their opposition to the church I made the decision not to invite them to attend. It was while I was standing in the baptismal tank that I caught an understanding of what it really means to be in God's family. I looked up and saw hundreds of adults and children standing around, the tank, smiling at me. There I understood how loved I was and felt like we were all in this together. I will never forget my baptism. It was powerful. I can still see that image in my mind today, the church community, encouraging me as I took a step in faith. A big and important step. When Pete asked if I accepted Jesus I was surprised to hear myself yell loudly, 'For sure!' The usual response was 'I do', but what came out was authentic and from the depths of my heart. The joy that welled up within me was beautiful. I was saying a big 'Yes!' to a life-changing commitment. I was aware of my decision and Jesus had started to become real to me. I was making the decision to tick off the enemy. My perspective had changed, it was a decision based on love and trust. I was learning about God and I started to believe what I was being taught. Revelation was birthed week after week in my heart. Change was happening. The victories were sweet. I held them tightly in my heart.

Step by step my life started to transform. Healing was evident as my mind became clearer. The voice bugged me occasionally, but I began to be conscious of an extraordinary silence. It felt strange to have a clear head, to be able to think. It was such an unfamiliar feeling that felt unusual at first. I had to learn to enjoy it and trust it. At times I was looking for it; wondering where it went. Pete spoke wisdom to me one day and said 'Angie let it go, don't try and find it otherwise you might be inviting back in.' I found this difficult because it had been there so long. I came to appreciate the sound of silence but it took some time to adjust. I never thought that I would be able to hear the voice of God. My mind was so full of other conversations. Conversations that were crude, profanity, screaming, yelling, trickery. Life had been chaos in my mind. I will never forget the first time that I knew God spoke to me. The word was: 'No eye has seen, No ear has heard,

No mind can conceive what God has prepared for those who love Him. I typed it out and told Dawn. I heard the voice of God and I was elated. I held onto that promise. God had a good plan for me. I trusted it one hundred percent. Pete was excited, as was Dawn. The breakthroughs that were happening were amazing. I also came to an understanding of why my healing wasn't immediate. Even as a Christian there was a huge pull to go back to the New Age. There were so many learnt behaviours and so many wrong beliefs entrenched in my mind and it took time to replace them with the truth of God's word. Without the months of prayer and counselling it was possible that I would have been unable to resist that strong pull back. I believe it was the grace of God that I did not get delivered immediately. God knew what was best.

....

I love this passage from Ecclesiastes.

There is a time for everything
And a season for every activity under the heavens:
A time to be born and a time to die,
A time to plant and a time to uproot,
A time to kill and a time to heal,

A time to tear down and a time to build,
A time to weep and a time to laugh,
A time to mourn and a time to dance,
A time to scatter stones and a time to gather them,
A time to embrace and a time to refrain from embracing,
A time to search and a time to give up,
A time to keep and a time to throw away,
A time to tear and a time to mend,
A time to be silent and a time to speak,
A time to love and a time to hate,
A time for war and a time for peace.

He has made everything beautiful in its time.

God has truly made everything beautiful in its time in my life. One of the miracles I treasure is a sane mind; to think and to have a conversation. I never take it for granted. There was also the miracle of the restoration of joy. I had to allow myself to experience joy. I felt uncomfortable with it for a while because it was so long since I'd experienced it. I tried to explain this to my doctor and he was concerned. He said, "Angie, we need to keep an eye on you to see if you have bipolar.' I spoke to Sallyanne about that and she told me not to accept that label. Now, every day is a gift. There are no words to truly express my gratitude for all He has done for me. I received a second chance, the ability to live an extra ordinary life, freedom and joy. The greatest gift, a childhood, to be parented by God himself, to be loved, honoured and adored. To experience favor, to come out from under the curse and live without the constant drama. It was never made up drama, it was real, but it was so constant. We would recover as a family from one traumatic event just to experience another. I don't live like that anymore. Life is a lot more peaceful. Jesus is the reason for that dramatic change in circumstances. I am protected, I am safe. I'm so grateful for those He sent into my world to stand with me to teach me that what is impossible for man is possible in Him. Anything is possible for those who believe. Miracles do happen! My life speaks of many miracles, but the greatest one is knowing Jesus. No greater love has anyone that this, that He lay down His life for His friends. Jesus is my best friend and I love Him.

During this process I was still required to see a psychiatrist as an outpatient. Dr Vanderbos had been gradually decreasing my medication and encouraged me to continue the counselling sessions with Peter and Sallyanne. He believed it was a good idea to work through the challenges that I had experienced with as much support as possible. He was obviously curious about the improvement in my mood and general mental health and one day he asked what had brought about the change. I told him it was due to the commitment I had made to Jesus. He acknowledged that the changes were miraculous given that my case notes showed I had been assessed as a patient who the doctors feared would eventually suicide. I was shocked to learn that my treating doctors had believed and wrote that up in my case notes. Their rationale for this incorrect prediction was that they had changed my medications schedule many times and saw that in every case I was not responding to the medication.

I remember Sallyanne asking me one day: 'Angie does the medication help remove the voice in any way, even slightly? I answered honestly, 'no'. She said 'This helps me to understand that this is a spiritual issue then because if you had schizophrenia the medication should help.' This conversation was a powerful moment in my heart and a leap towards my freedom. We knew together that this was a spiritual issue. I had had that consistent perspective the whole time but finally someone else trusted that too. I was relieved and felt stronger after this conversation. I often tried to explain that to my treating doctors hoping they would understand. They never did. Every time I tried to explain that I knew how the voice came in, during the ritual that night, they just increased my meds and kept me detained in the hospital. They refused to listen.

The healing that I experienced represents to me the extent of the miraculous in my life. When the medical world said 'death', God said 'life'.

About a year after my baptism I made the decision to come off all medication. This was a step of faith for me because the anti-depressants and anti-psychotics had at least given me a sense of security. The anti-depressant did help and provide a benefit during counselling. Medical science is not the complete answer, but it can be a useful tool in mental health issues. I took the medication because of the trauma I faced. I had become depressed, I had been traumatised by evil and I believed that even if it helped me one per cent, it was beneficial for a season. Initially, I was nervous about coming off medication, but something in my heart said 'it's time'. I asked Sallyanne, who is a qualified psychologist, to keep an eye on me and tell me if she noticed any deterioration in my mood or behaviour. I wanted to be accountable, I needed to know that someone had my back. From that day to the present I have not needed to resume those medications.

Thinking that my doctor might try to talk me out of my decision, it was six months before I told my psychiatrist about coming off the medications. He was not happy at all and extremely concerned about that decision. He did acknowledge there had been no deterioration in my well-being without medication, instead I had improved. I have not had another psychiatric appointment since.

FOUR

COUNTING THE COST

There was a price to pay for giving my life and trusting God. I had to let go of my old ways. Part of that cost was Marko announcing that he was leaving me, saying he had only waited until I was stronger. From a Christian viewpoint our relationship had always been extremely dysfunctional, but for us we were accountable to what we knew: living together outside of marriage, smoking marijuana and drinking heavily on weekends. That's just what you did to deal with trauma and alleviate the pressures of life. I'm not justifying or advocating these things I'm simply acknowledging the choices and decisions people make outside of faith in God. Life without God is where co-dependent relationships and addictions are formed. It's called survival. We all worship something: the bottle, drugs, sex, material wealth. In order to cope, my husband and I used all of those things at different times. There came a time when none of those coping mechanisms were the answer for me. I remember clearly the day that I threw my pipe way and with it the small amount of marajuana that I had in a small money bag. I emptied the contents in the toilet and flushed it. Marko would have freaked out if he saw that, he would have become angry because he would have wanted to smoke it. I threw the pipe in the bin. It was a stand. I had to do it. It was like drawing a good boundary around my life. I chose a different way to deal with my pain and dope wasn't right anymore. Looking back, the breaking point for our marriage was my breakdown after the loss of our baby. Marko supported me in the most incredible ways and stood by me in my darkest hour. There is no way I could have handled a separation at that time. I appreciated his respect in waiting until I could. He waited until I was emotionally stronger.

The grief of the separation was overwhelming. I cried a river of tears. I kept remembering Marko's promises during the dark times, his promise that he would never leave me. Why leave me now when I was getting better? I knew I had made choices and decisions that affected our relationship and I took responsibility for them, however I made a covenant with him in marriage and I expected to have a family and spend the rest of our lives together. I did not intentionally create the chaos, I simply did not foresee the ramifications of my choices.

My husband was a remarkable man. I remained faithful and positioned myself for the miraculous. How could I not, after everything God was doing in my life? I'm grateful for the peace that I experienced during that time. In the natural, reconciliation seemed unlikely, but in God I saw the impossible so I stood in faith and prayed and trusted. Clearly I remember; a day that I was driving south for a meeting and I saw a car like Marko's. It got my attention and I clearly heard: 'I am releasing you from this calibre of people.' I instantly thought of Marko. That week when I went to the letter box I received court documents and was served a notice of divorce. Again, I understood that it was the right decision, because I had been pre-warned of the impending divorce and I did not contest it in any way. I let him go without conflict. Yes, there were many tears. Unfortunately, things don't always turn out the way we hope they will. It highlights our ability to choose; our free will. The divorce was a huge disappointment and I don't know how people survive divorce and relationship breakdown outside of relationship with God. I knew how I wanted to handle it and I'm grateful I had the peace and love not to create a mess. I didn't want it to become ugly, I refused to punish him by manipulation or control. I chose to trust God and stand in faith.

Hindsight is an interesting thing. I learned so much from the pain of this experience. It's amazing how negative experiences can bring so much understanding and insight if we allow it. I was able to look back on the ten years we were together and appreciate the love and relationship that was so special. We had walked through so much adversity together and came out of it with respect and genuine love for each other, even as non-Christians. Without those experiences I would not be the woman I am today. I realised that I chose a different path, I chose a road of spiritual truth. Marko never chose that path and I understood that my choice had changed everything. How could I punish him for that?

There was a powerful experience that I had about a week before Marko left that helped me through this difficult season. I was at mum's house and I had this thought in my head: 'If you had to choose between Marko or God, who would you choose?' I remember thinking: gee that is a strange thought!', but I considered the question. Speaking to myself, I said that I would choose God! I continued on without considering the question again until Marko left. The day he announced that he was leaving me I was pretty distressed and crying. Marko had just left the house and I heard a little whisper in my heart, 'you chose God remember?' My heart and my head understood it. I knew God was close and I knew I had a part to play in the decision that had been made. I chose God. It changed my whole perspective. God had my back and prepared me for what was ahead.

God took my mess and gave me a message of hope, of love, of forgiveness, of truth. This is what qualifies me to speak, to love passionately, to understand, to live beyond myself. Every traumatic event in my life serves a purpose today. It gives me insight and understanding into situations people face in life. You see, I believe every person has an amazing ability to live in destiny, in the plan ordained for them by my creator. This is made possible by obedience. Even in my darkest hour I discovered that when we are in a place beyond our ability to endure we have the opportunity to experience a love beyond our ability to express.

It was time for the next step and a deeper level of healing.

ANGIE AMUSO

IN HIS STEPS

There was nobody to show me how
The darkness that encompassed me, suppressed the truth...ME!
'I couldn't see the footprints in the sand'.
Fearful, lost, scared and confused
The intense isolation within ebbed away at my confidence, my hope and my dreams.
I knew, I knew in the depths of my soul
There was more
The battles that raged within, the inner conflict warred silently attacking my heart, mind and soul
The outside world had no idea of the devastation I was experiencing internally
Survival was the only way I knew how
My footprints trod sporadically, my path uncertain
Escapism, yes to numb the reality of truth
My life was insane, no direction, no understanding
Faith? Hey where was God...in this mess?
I knew that I was a sinner, I knew that for sure
That scared the living jeebies out of me That made me more fearful Confession...communion...religion... Confirmation...

Scary stuff, not my choice!
Drugs, alcohol, dysfunctional to the max, that's my life story, there's more Suicide...divorce...abuse- take your pick Unheard of oppression.
Victim, yep...circumstance...insane Hopeless. Helpless yep That's my story, but there's more Truth, light, sanity, found, DELIVERED, SIGNED AND SEALED, Redeemed by my Saviour
He died for a monkey like me
My God is into the miraculous

As I reviewed my journey, my old life, I cried so many tears. I was a broken woman... broken for all the right reasons. I entered into a season of letting go of everything...... laying down the old memories that I knew, the old thought patterns, letting go of the lies I believed, healing of my memories of the past... the trauma... healing of my soul.... I never really had the emotional space 'to go there' before.

I poured out my heart to heaven in a childlike way and He listened to my cry in a way that was intimate like I'd never felt before. I had to learn to feel comfortable with intimacy, I didn't learn this as a child. I could sense Him saying to me daily: 'Your perspective is so important to me.' Physically, emotionally and spiritually it felt as though I was running a marathon. My muscles were burning, and my heart was racing. I was giving everything that I had to this transformational process, and when I thought I couldn't take another step I entered a place where I understood His grace and how His power is made perfect in my weakness. He carried me, and held me tight. He protected me and showered me with words of love... 'your mine, I will never let go.' That's when a new energy came, I accessed His power. My stride looked different, my head was held high, shoulders back, running in confidence, but not a confidence in self. The confidence is that it is my race to win, freedom was mine to access. I just had to believe. I am heaven's kid and I have to win. I have to discover who I am, and who He is; I want authentic relationship. Trust and confidence grew as I held this truth. The enemy tried hard to derail me but I rejected the lies and I held on to the truth of heaven. I heard the whisper of heaven saying: 'your perspective is important to me.' That was the revelation that fed my soul and my mind started to believe that word and my heart grew stronger. Heaven cared about my thoughts, He truly cared about my heart. It was awesome and it was difficult. It was difficult because my mind didn't really understand it... the experience of a daddy's love had to be learnt by experience. That's why the daily reassurance came and as I continued to let my guard down, the wall in my heart was dismantled brick by brick. The wall that was there to protect my heart was slowly being removed... freedom was closer.

No one else saw the full picture of the pain of this season. I spared them that. Mainly because I could not articulate it. I bare my soul now to tell the truth of this journey. I was saved when I accepted Jesus however there was an important process that needed to take place: deliverance from my past. Inside-out heart transformation can take you to the edge and it's important to have support in place before you start. I did a lot of this alone, just me and God – and trust me, it wasn't pretty. It felt as though it was a messy process. By messy I mean I cried a lot, I felt a lot of pain, I talked it through with him and by faith I said I need a daddy's love. I don't want a distant God. I have been taught that you want relationship and I will do whatever it takes to find that. I decided that I wanted to learn to trust a daddy's love and it was painful because it highlighted my lack. I had to start and the developmental stage of an infant, trust versus mistrust, is the first milestone in any relationship. A daddy's love is powerful and a lack of it, destructive. I was peering into two worlds and I daily chose to give him my hand, give him my heart and allow the disfunction that hid in my soul to be healed. If someone mentioned the word dad in a conversation, my heart would freak out, fear gripped me, my body became tense and my mind flashed back to the past. My mind wanted to trust that a daddy's love was safe but my subconscious screamed a different story. I didn't want to listen to that pain, but it was so loud I couldn't ignore it. It was real, I lived it. It needed to be healed but it was not an overnight process. I was committed to trusting the necessary developmental stages that were required because I knew it was important for my future and my freedom. Much of the time we unintentionally view God by our interaction and experience with our own fathers and much of the time we are unaware that we are projecting their truth or our bad experience onto Him. For me, my relationship with Daddy God would never be healthy if I did that. That's why this process was so important. No more skeletons in the cupboard. The light exposed the darkness, and it was uncomfortable to see. The learnt behaviours, the thoughts, the fears, the issues that don't line up with living a successful life with Jesus. An important key that kept me on track was that there were times when God allowed me to rest. Unconditional love always filled my heart and soul, I knew it was ok to reflect on how far I had come in Him. A valuable key... to be able to see the victories. It strengthened my journey as I held these close to my heart. Deep down I knew I would make it. Death to the old to make way for the new. He knew I needed rest and time to recover. The foundations needed time to set and after that I would climb faster than expected. There were seasons of exponential growth; as I fed on revelational truth. I fed on the simple truths of a daddy's love day after day, learning truths that I did not experience as a baby or young girl. This was an incredibly powerful and intimate season. I knew He was watching, and I knew

He was proud of me. I liked that thought, a daddy proud of me! Wow, that was a strengthening agent. I recall that I would be in worship on a Sunday at church, singing my guts out, my soul abandoned to the natural realm. Looking to heaven and giving him glory, I was telling my daddy that i trusted him through song. I would feel things flying off me, things that were on my head. I knew it was something bad leaving and I was worried for others. My heart cried: 'God please don't let that jump on anyone else here.' I felt it leave the spiritual atmosphere, I was freer from that moment on in time, not trying to be freer, just by allowing my heart to connect with His. I was starting to see resilience growing as I faced the challenges of life differently; and this was bringing new levels of understanding and revelation. Revelation applied to experience is powerful. I was creating a new history; reordering a legacy according to kingdom values. I was telling the darkness that it no longer had a place in my life. I also believed my family would prosper from my success. I was learning that I was no longer a slave to fear; to the lies; to voice of evil. I held onto the truth and I knew that this process was not just for me but would affect a generation - those that would take the baton and run ahead of me. It broke generational ties and influences that had cursed our family. The enemy was angry because I was taking ground but in my heart I drew boundary lines of love around our family and created space for the spirit to work. I screamed at the devil 'my family is off-limits, I will do whatever it takes for our freedom.' This created conflict in the natural as the forces of evil fought hard against the will of God. The attacks were difficult, but it was my fight to win. You see when you come into Jesus the way I did, you learn something really powerful: you learn to fight. Salvation is a gift but when I made a decision for Christ, a war broke out that nearly took me out. I don't share this to scare you but to encourage you. The very thing that tried to take me out was what God gave me to rule over. Authority is something you can learn. You learn to partner with God and it is important for your ultimate success, as well as the success of others. Learning to fight God's way is very different to fighting in a natural way. It is vital that we learn to hear His voice and allow Him to give us the strategy for breakthrough. Physical strength in and of itself will not bring the breakthrough. His lead, His directional word each and every time is the key. It was an important lesson that I learnt early on.

In the next season heaven took me to a place of stillness. I sat at the feet of Jesus and He ministered to me in amazing ways. In these times I ministered to Him, too. That is, I continued to share the cry of my heart and spoke honestly, and told Him exactly how I was feeling. It took time to have the confidence to do that until I reached a place where I realised that He knew it all anyway.

He had been wooing me into this place for some time. Slowly, slowly he wooed me. Leading me ever so gently into a deeper levels of intimacy. I was being totally, 100 percent real about my emotions for the first time in my life. I entered into a 'real' relationship with Jesus in this season. Honesty, vulnerability and transparency was something that I came to enjoy with him each night and we would have intimate discussions about the truth that lived within my heart and soul. As I told Him the truth about my experiences and pain, healing came quicker. I spoke and He talked back to me. I heard His perspective clearly. I created a space just for him, no one else was allowed here. This was deep and it was safe. I took the risk and I am glad I did. It had a transforming effect that was to affect my life forever.

In this season I became a high school chaplain and I was well liked and respected. I connected really well with everyone in the school community and was able to be incredibly involved in the curriculum as well as the routine responsibilities within the school. Students regularly visited my office and I was committed to learning under the Holy Spirit's watchful eye. One day I was sitting in my office and the recess bell rang. God said to me very clearly 'stay in your office.' I said, 'stay in my office, really? There are 500 students out there and you want me to sit here, really? 'I had to be sure this was God speaking! Sure enough, He clearly said yes, sit here please. So I did. I grabbed a Bible study that was sitting on my desk. It had been given to me by a Christian staff member earlier that day. Next minute a student, Daryl, came to my office. Standing at my door he said 'Hi Angie, how are you? what are you doing?' I think he was waiting for me to go out to the students, because this was part of my usual routine. I said 'Oh I'm reading a bible study'. He said 'what is a bible study?' I said it was about learning about God. I always maintained a very honest and open approach to my students. He said 'oh ok' and left. I was asking God for permission to leave the room and go and catch up with some of the students in the yard when Daryl came back to the doorway with a friend; he said 'Angie can we do a bible study?' I smiled and understood why my obedience was important. I said sure. I will look into it.

I spoke to the principal and explained what had happened. She was more than happy for the students to get permission from their parents and come along to my church after school. I started the bible study group that next week with the two students that asked, they spread word through the school and there were other students interested also. The first week I had a conversation to them about making a decision to follow Jesus. I explained that there was a door on their heart and only one person had access to that door - them. I explained that Jesus was standing at the door and was knocking. He was asking for an invitation into their heart. They both responded when I asked 'What do you want to do? Do you want to allow Jesus access to your heart? they both eagerly said yes! They gave their heart to heaven, with me right there and then. I was so excited. We also started a lunchtime group for the students at the public high school, as well as the group after church. The students would walk up the hill each week to church. The group was fun with a strong relational focus. Both groups were thriving with students.

At the same time, I was also volunteering my time in the local public hospital. I believed that it was important to support the community in times of distress. I had a small team and we did weekly visits, providing a patient care and support service. On a Friday night we worked in the emergency section and where permissible, made a cup of coffee or tea for the patients, staff and support people. We sat alongside people in our community who were suffering. The staff would ask me to go and spend time with suicidal patients and people in distress. My team and I were given a swipe card and had access to staff only areas of the hospital. I loved this work, I loved my team and it was here that I overcame any fear I previously had about God being able to use my life for the greater good. I was shocked at the favour. I also visited psychiatric wards and these frightened me at first. Not the patients, but the staff. I hated the stigma that they had placed on my life. I continued with the visits though because I knew it was a fear that I had to overcome. God was healing the shame of my past experiences during this season. He destroyed any stigma I felt that had been associated with mental health issues of my past. I recall on a Friday night one of the staff pulling me aside and asking me to go and visit one of the patients who were in distress, having suicidal thoughts. Tracey was a street kid, 16 years old. She lived on the streets of Adelaide or in youth shelters if they were available. She had been on the streets since the age of 11. She knew the system well, she had no contact with her family at all, she hadn't seen them for years. I walked into Tracey's cubicle gently asking for permission to enter. She said 'yeah if you want?' She was clearly ticked off, and started yelling and telling me how bad her treatment and care was. I explained that I was there to help out. She asked; if I could take her out for a smoke? I asked if I did; would she run away? She promised that she wouldn't. I had to trust her word. From my previous youth work experience, I understood that you have to offer trust. Its powerful; sometimes teenagers live in the expectation of the adults in their world. I said 'well if the nurses agree then I'm happy too.' The nurses agreed and I won her trust out there. As she smoked a few cigarettes, we talked. It was her talking mainly and I learnt to listen carefully. She loved the attention and my time, that was obvious. I spent the rest of the night chatting with her and completed my shift at twelve o'clock that night. I went home and prayed and thanked God for the connection, and the opportunity to build with this young lady, I thought that she was sweet, I liked her. I saw through the rough exterior and accessed a love that only a mummy would know. Then next day it was in my thoughts to catch up with her again, so I did what I didn't normally didn't do. I went to the hospital into the emergency ward and spoke to the triage nurse and asked if I could see Tracey again. I was really well known and trusted by the staff team, doctors and the Mental Health Assessment Team. Over time the service that I had pioneered had gained much credibility, the feedback was really encouraging. We made a difference. My team loved their work, they were brilliant to lead.

As I entered into Tracey's cubicle, the same one as the previous night, she started yelling 'nobody cares about me....' I stopped her abruptly when I said respectfully 'Well I'm here aren't I?' She didn't know what to say. Then she said 'yeah' and calmed down. Because I took her for a smoke the previous night, and she didn't run away, the staff trusted her to go outside for a smoke with me again. That was her first request after our initial conversation. I think the stress of needing a smoke was part of the issue on my arrival. On our way out to the smoking area, two of the Mental Health Assessment Team called me over to discuss Tracey. Then they shocked me with this question: 'Angie, can you help this kid? if we give her to you, can you help her. We can try and get funding if you can? We have tried everything and it's not working.' I immediately said 'Yes, I can help her, I will take her.' I explained to Tracey that the Mental Health Team asked if I could help them to provide support. I asked her if she wanted me to help out. She agreed and was pleased with that decision. I had won her trust big time! Tracey was admitted to an open psychiatric ward by the Mental Health Team that day, my name was placed on her notes and I was officially allowed to be informed of the decisions and be a part of her support team. I felt comfortable with that decision. I left Tracey in the hospital reassuring her that I would return. I told Pete about Tracey. Pete was the person who oversaw my work, he was a friend and someone I trusted deeply. We had walked through much difficulty together, Sally-anne also. If I ever needed advice that's who I spoke too. Pete said that he would pray for Tracey and encouraged me to continue the relationship.

The next day I had Tracey heavily on my heart. I heard the spirit say 'today I want you to talk to Tracey about me, I want you to introduce her to me?' I wasn't sure how I was going to do that, but I knew heaven's agenda. I made my way to the Mental Health Ward not knowing how to start the conversation. When I met her in the foyer I asked if she wanted to come outside and sit on the grass. Mental Health wards are dark; they have heavy atmospheres. There is a lot of spiritual darkness - it's one of the darkest places in the community. I wanted to create and bring her into a more pleasant atmosphere. She agreed and we headed over to the lawn space; a space I myself as a patient had laid on. It was there that I asked Dawn what the 'Our Father' prayer really meant. That was about four years previously. Tracey sat down and I said 'Tracey there is something that I need to talk to you about.' Tracey said 'I know.' I said 'You know?' She said 'yeah I had a dream last night, and in the dream a man came to me and told me to trust you. I need to give my heart to Jesus.' I nearly fell over. I clarified what I heard 'You had a dream last night, and you want to give your heart to Jesus?' 'Yes I do' she said passionately, so I led her in a simple prayer asking for Jesus to come into her heart. I was overjoyed. The visit was full of hope and within a couple days Tracey was discharged from hospital. I invited her to church and I introduced her to many people. Pete and Sallyanne were one of the first introductions. Tracey came to my house the first night for dinner. One of the couples in the church were also coming for tea that night and at the end of the night they organised for Tracey to stay in a hotel.

Pete asked around and a couple in the church offered to have Tracey stay with them. They were strong in love and looked after her well. I was praying for accommodation that was permanent for her and one day she spoke to me on the phone and said 'Do you know what Angie; I have to pray for accommodation.' I said 'Great; prayer is powerful.' The very next day Tracey received a call saying she had received accommodation. She was excited that God heard her prayer. Faith was growing, every need she had was sorted. Her life was transforming. She became reconnected to her family. It was such a beautiful process to watch. Tracey became part of the Christian family, she developed friendships and grew to love me as a mother. I remember the day that I had to discipline her; it was something little, her swearing; but I knew she would lose credibility if she continued to us the F bomb. I organised a coffee date and carefully talked to her about her language. She responded maturely and made the adjustment immediately. I was thankful it went so well. Many months later she said that the day I earned the most respect from her was that day, the day I asked her not to use the F bomb. She said 'when you did that, I knew you loved me.' Our kids want and need healthy boundaries and it teaches them that we love them. This insight came from a kid who had lived on the streets from the age of eleven where she didn't have boundaries; she didn't have a parental love; she didn't take orders from anyone. She did her own thing, the way she wanted and had little respect for authority. This was a huge miracle: her ability to be loved. The church family taught her unconditional love and acceptance and it was powerful to observe. Tracey's journey is ongoing, as she continues to journey with God and walk through the choices and decisions that life brings. We all chose daily, who we follow.

....

Hindsight is beautiful. Looking back, I can see how quick my spiritual growth was in this season, behind the scenes, behind closed doors. Memories had been healed. I had been ridiculed for being too sensitive, too slow, not good enough, not as good as... whoever. These are the places where self-protection starts and walls go up. Words can devastate the mind and the emotions, the soul. Facing this pain head-on was an important part of the process during this season of healing. God helped me understand that facing the hurtful reality of the negative experiences that wounded my soul was not about blaming or accusation, it was about allowing the pain of the past to be healed. It was to be a catalyst for growth and health. I grew quickly during this process. As the lies were being exposed and washed away and the truth had opportunity to penetrate. I started to realise who I belonged to. I was heaven's kid. Revelation from the soul of heaven continued to flood my soul. The spoken word of God, and experience of heaven's love, was a daily occurrence. I gave out the love I received. It was God's faithfulness and measures of love deposited daily that gave me the ability to continue to care for the kids and some of their families that he placed in my world. Faith grew in my heart. Consistently seeing the reality of God doing what is impossible, seeing the miraculous in my life and in the lives of others was powerful. It stirred my faith to believe for greater things.

You can only take someone as far as you have been. Our subconscious memory is powerful and if we don't stop and look at the areas that are not healthy, we may continue to repeat cycles of disfunction. I realised later, upon reflection, that because my influence in the community was growing and my influence in the lives of others was growing rapidly, it was important for the areas of my heart that were still damaged to be healed. It was as if the kids that I was working with, their level of disfunction was somehow exposing my heart. I was faced with looking at things from a parenting perspective and my reality, my previous experience clashed with heaven's way. It was extremely confrontational and no one was aware that I was struggling in this season except Pete and Sallyanne. I talked with Sallyanne during this season of renewal. I held onto the hand of Jesus and I processed through the pain. I came to know this place well.

ANGIE AMUSO

THE TURNING POINT

The door was locked shut, dead bolted with a latch
On the other side was fear, insecurity, intense grief beyond words
Darkness hid, suppressing the truth of my soul
Years of unresolved pain
Unintentionally outworking themselves into yesterday
I walked into a level of freedom and light when I met Jesus
However I chose to surrender only in part, I was scared to unlock that door
Coz I knew what hid there
Guilt, shame, a stark reality of truth that I just didn't want to face
Coz I knew it would hurt
Jesus kept knocking, please let me in
'I have come to set you free, freedom that will take your breathe away'.
As the walls came down, Jesus slowly took a brick away one at a time.
Because that wall that I had built around my heart, was big, too much for me to handle.

Courage Over Adversity

I felt brave, yes Jesus come in, I want every promise that you have for me,
I want that freedom that was the cry of my heart
Slowly I unlocked that door, one lock at a time.
His light shone into that darkness as the door opened
Denial could no longer live there; Grace moved in instead
This type of reality is confrontational; I'm not going to minimalise this process
Yes it hurts, its uncomfortable, seems unbearable at times
My Jesus He is the anchor to my soul
His word, His promises, His love and devotion to me
Was what held me during the trials of truth?
He carries me in the darkness and leads me into the light
My future is bright...my saviour told me
I trust Him... He's my everything

FIVE

THE FATHER-HEART OF GOD

I needed to learn about a daddy's heart. I was terrified of my natural dad. I only have one photo today with him holding me. I don't recall dad holding me often, he left that to mum. One of my favourite memories was the family gathering for the night to watch television. I would sit on mum's lap and she would wrap her arms around me. I would rest on her chest and hear her heart beat and hear and feel her every breath. Being an emotional child, I felt everything like it was an atmosphere around me. This is what created the chaos in my heart. I remember laying on mum one night and noticing the whip in the corner of the room. If we stepped out of line, this was our new punishment. I was trusting mum was going to speak up, I didn't want to be punished; I knew it would hurt. I got it once and once only, I think mum put a stop to it.

I was now thirty-two and God wanted my trust. I had to replace my dad's love with God's love. I wanted to in my head, but my heart would panic. Pete was a man that entered into my life as an authority figure and I trusted him, but not consciously as a daughter but as a friend. He was my leader.

I used this time to face my fears and step into a relationship with God as a daddy. Today everything I do is from drawing close to the experience of daddy God's love and fall more in love with Him. During that time, I was growing dependent on His peace and He carried me in the most intimate ways. His tangible embrace kept me. There was no other choice that I wanted but to let it be a place of surrender and humility.

It was in this season that I understood me, the effects of my history, and the effects on my soul. It really is the truth that sets us free. I understood the root issues, where fear, insecurity and doubt had crept in. Sometimes it felt like I was dying, and I guess I was: dying to old thought patterns, fears and belief systems that didn't line up with a daddy's love. I know he carried me through every stage of this transformation as I let go of the understanding of a natural father's love and allowed Him to replace it with a real daddy's love. I sensed heaven cheering me on. When we give trust to God, He proves trust worthy. Even today, Daddy God is very gentle with me. Not harsh, not abrupt, never impatient, and definitely never angry. He respects our journey together and it's priceless to him. He won't allow any man to hurt or damage me. He protects me fiercely from those that intend me harm. He made a commitment to me, the same that I made to Him. To give me His life. I believe my trust is very important to Him. He puts a high value on it and does all He can to protect it. When He disciplines me, He takes me into His arms and holds me close and squeezes me and says 'Little one, you're better than that.' Then I cry to Him, and tell him I'm sorry. He gives me the strength to make the changes. It's easy in Him. It's intimate and its deep. We talk and talk and talk and talk every day. He likes me and I like Him. We do everything together. Inseparable. I am loved and I know it. I ask him how he is, how he is feeling and He speaks to me as a friend, intimately and honestly. He loves to be with me; He told me, and that's the only place I want to be, in His embrace. I live this reality day after day after day. It just gets deeper; it just gets better.

The spiritual opposition to this season was intense as Satan, my enemy also saw my life beginning to show fruit. He hates it when we discover who we are, who we belong to. I stood firm on the prophetic promises that had been spoken over me. In this season I was asked to be a leader in my church. A leader? I questioned. But I have been divorced? Pete said 'Angie you have clean hands, you did nothing wrong.' I was shocked and didn't see that promotion coming.

I had many opportunities to lead people to Christ during this season. The daily process I committed to behind the scenes of my life was what qualified me to bear more fruit. My faith, character, attitudes, authority and convictions were tested as God breathed His word and Spirit into the dead areas. The revelation of God's love and grace revolutionised me. I knew that in the future people would be radically touched by what I was learning now. How to embrace a daddy's heart. This is what gave me the courage to persevere. It is the big picture of what God has promised. As the lies left, love crept into my heart and soul.

I often asked God why? Why would any person go through such a high level of oppression and opposition as I did? I believe that, in part, it is because of the call upon my life. As a first generation Christian - as I am in my family - a warrior spirit is a necessity. I had to constantly keep reminding myself of the bigger picture. One day I would birth a child of my own, who deserved the right to be born into freedom. I didn't want my children to fight a fight that I refused to. This was the inspiration at times for fighting these internal battles: my reward, freedom and a legacy.

I had to remember that there are thousands of people locked up in psychiatric hospitals, trapped in the darkness of mind, heart and soul and with no concept of the great love of God. For such people, death seems the only option, and outside of Christ, it is. Understanding both sides gives powerful insight - it gives the ability to see the possibility of lives transformed when no one else would believe it. My motivation for sharing is to break down the fear and stereotypical misconceptions in society about mental health. My heart is for God to use my testimony to help others understand. With knowledge comes power. Love is the vehicle in which power is expressed. Our community and its children need love; the option outside of Heaven's intervention will lead ultimately to death for some. I know the solution. We hold the key. we hold the ability to keep people locked in darkness or can choose to use the key to set them free. We live once. We all have a choice to make. The long road was my choice. I stand by that decision today and allow the heart of a good Daddy lead all the way.

ANGIE AMUSO

I REMEMBER

My heart is broken, such sorrow,
I'm exhausted know my Saviour
Why such sadness?
I contemplate as tears stream down my face.
This is tough...this process
I feel sad, the tears flow, I consciously access,' where am I at?'
I remember your word, your truth
To be honest, I really don't understand
This is a place where faith must live
Do I doubt my God? No!
I remember that vision...the lock...it's open
I trust Him
I trust Him with all of my heart
I stand
I remember His touch
In Him, He holds me
His lead, His words
I follow
He understands
'I remember that dream

Courage Over Adversity

His tear.
I didn't understand
Thank you my Lord, I do now
Your tear, heals my soul
I have a choice
I choose to praise you my Lord
I love you with all that I am.
I surrender

Over many years a dismantling continued to take place in my life. Foundational structures that didn't line up with a Daddy's love were uprooted, pulled down, overthrown and totally destroyed. Once again, my heart was again undergoing major surgery without anaesthetic.

More intense spiritual opposition began to take place. I was starting to understand and walk intimately in a daddy's love and the enemy was ticked off! He tried every trick in the book to take me out. People had no idea of what was happening in my world. Again I did not know how to tell them because I did not fully understand it myself. It is not an exaggeration when I say war broke out. It was a new level of opposition that I had not faced as a Christian. I questioned if I could really be saved if I faced this type of opposition? I questioned 'Is the enemy trying to steal my testimony?' I had to tell myself, 'No! I won't allow it!' In such circumstances faith formed and strengthened in my core. It was a place of total surrender and dependency on Him. Again I chose to I sit on my daddy's lap and enter into a childlike intimacy and vulnerability and I allowed Him to teach me how to receive from Him. During the war I took a lot of deep breaths! I read God's word. I prayed a lot of crisis prayers; 'Help me, Lord, I'm about to die!' (I actually sensed His smiling reply, 'Yep, I know!'). I learnt that he doesn't panic like we do because He knows what is being achieved in these times of war. I learnt that life was never going to be the same again. A daddy's love would be etched in my heart forever. His protection, His provision.

Despite the war, my life was effective. I was working into the highest level of need within our community with great success in Him. I remember a call from the hospital asking: 'Angie can you help?...... there's a need, domestic violence, a young lady has been bashed by her partner.' It was serious. 'Yes', I said... 'I want to help, what can I do?' One thought, conscious thought when there is a need. 'I have the answer... His name is Jesus... I have the Solution... A daddy's love... Yep what can I do...?' A call...for a patient involved in a domestic violence situation; a follow up phone call would be good, 'sure thing; I'll go one more step than that, I want to be there, support is important. I asked 'can I offer her a ride to her accommodation?'. My heart said I want to show her that people do care, there is a love that is real, that's available, the truth... I was given the details on where I was to pick her up and I drove to the hospital with a confidence, a knowing that I was in His will. I met her, her face beaten, her head bandaged, black eyes, extremely bloodshot, many broken fingers in splints, the physical pain and scars obvious. I knew the pain was much deeper, the hidden scars that remain when the physical blows healed. The outside world would have no idea of her insane life. There was a gentleness, a receptiveness. She is special, precious, I thought. She felt safe and I felt unusually relaxed, and comfortable. It was grace on me to do what was needed. I felt a compassionate love for her. , She didn't want sympathy... she had a need and she was reasonably comfortable for having just met me, a stranger. I considered it a privilege to help support her in any way I could. As we stepped outside the hospital, she nervously looked around. I nodded, and with a reassuring smile I gestured with my hand for her to make her way to my car, that was parked just a few steps away. I thought- 'hopefully she will feel safer there.' We talked as I drove and I asked open-ended questions with caution. She gave me insight into some of her world. I was amazed... her resilience through the pain she was enduring, it was encouraging to me, and it spoke of a grace on her life. As she spoke, I was able to offer encouragement. She explained that she understood that she needed to make changes in her life, she understood the need to be safe. I said there's hope, always hope, never give up, never ever. She spoke of her children; they were her hope. We drove for about fifteen minutes till we reached our destination, a hotel room made available by a women's shelter. We booked her in and then I walked her to her room, upstairs... room 11. I carried two small bags of groceries, with a few home cooked meals. She was tired, so I gave her my details and offered coffee if she needed company. I explained that we could provide counselling support if she wanted it. I gave her a hug, tears filled her eyes and I said I will be praying for you as she gently pressed her shoulders in to receive a tighter hug. She was obviously thankful and she smiled and waved goodbye as I left her. I hoped that she would ring me but she didn't. I tried to contact her, but she had checked out. I prayed a passionate prayer, the most valuable gift I could give her. I knew she needed my Jesus, His love, His truth. I believed and stood in faith for her salvation, I wonder how she is.

What a privilege. Every person is a gift to us, a life so important to God. I believe in miracles. She deserves so much more than the pain of enduring a beating like that. Her life is so precious. How, why? I don't understand. How can I understand, I haven't walked her journey, her life. I don't stand in judgment, no, I want to help. I choose to love, and be part of the solution and not part of the problem. She needs my prayers and ultimately to feel the embrace of my Heavenly Father. She is his child.

About two weeks later... the news caught my attention... person found murdered in her house... I felt uneasy... domestic violence... I felt even more uneasy as my thoughts flashed back to the call for help. There were some similarities, suburb... the truth was I didn't know. I rationalized it, I prayed she was ok. My heart was trying to convince my emotions that it was just a coincidence. I felt a nagging feeling that would not leave me. I wanted to watch the late night news to see if there was any more information. The report was similar, unidentified woman found dead, domestic violence.

I was restless that night, I couldn't sleep. Tossing and turning, something was troubling me. My thoughts flashed back to the domestic violence report.

Then I had this thought that brought an incredible peace and importantly, perspective. Sometimes God shows us mercy by taking us out of situations. He takes us out, to take us into Him. Maybe, just maybe, this was an act of grace and mercy. God's way of taking this woman out of a horrific, traumatic life situation. I would imagine, I could only imagine, the cry of this young woman's heart as she received a beating that bad. I prayed that her cry was 'God please help'. A crisis prayer in a moment like that would be an appropriate response. And, in God's mercy, taking her out of the situation may have been the best possible outcome, the most amazing outcome. Reconciled to Him, in Glory, no pain, no suffering, safe in his arms. This thought brought reassurance, built a faith in my heart and an understanding that sometimes things are not always black and white. God knows best. His way is perfect. He sees the beginning and the end.

Then my thoughts focused on the cross. Our Jesus died for the victim, and he died for the perpetrator, the murderer, in this situation. The perpetrator took her life in the natural but at the end of the day, every day of her life was given by God. Everything is subject to His authority. I hoped that in her last moments, she cried out to Him for help. Our Jesus, he endured a beating that was so great that he was beaten beyond recognition. Persecuted, flogged, spat on, insulted and betrayed. He endured the most painful, excruciating death, crucifixion, death on a cross. Jesus suffered excruciating pain at the hands of men like no other man will experience in History. He did it because he thought this lady who died by domestic violence was worth it. He died so that she could live. Possibly people watching the 5 O'clock news, wondered where God was, or why God would allow this situation to occur, and why he allowed her to suffer a violent death like this. I wonder if they considered the fact that God gave His son, for this precious life and theirs. And maybe, just maybe it was a divine act of grace and mercy.

That night I went to mum's. I was there for about five minutes and she said: 'Hey Angie did you hear about the young lady that was murdered?' I knew what she was going to say, I felt uneasy and said 'yeah, do you know her name?' She repeated the surname of the lady I recently met and my thoughts were confirmed: yes, it was her. I went into shock for a moment; I had chills through my body. I wanted to hear it for myself because I needed it confirmed by the news report. I sat down to watch the news and eventually they came to her story. This terrible revelation had gone from my heart to my head... it was confirmed.

I knew God was teaching me through this situation. He directs and orders my steps and I give him that permission. I had the privilege of supporting this young lady in her last few days on Earth. This meeting was no coincidence. I was devastated by this news but I am truly thankful for having met this lady, my life enriched by having met her. I am sad. Yes, there is a sadness in my heart, however there is also a peace. I am walking in His will.

....

My relationship with daddy God grew in powerful ways during this season. I grew to trust Him for myself and for others. He doesn't wait until we are perfectly healed and whole before He chooses to use us for His plans and purposes. In some ways my freedom came through giving. I walked closely with His heart through these seasons and he taught me things that a church guest speaker could not. This lady who died at the hands of her husband, my students, Tracey, the people heaven brought into my world. They became my greatest teachers and they taught me about love. They taught me how to fight for another's freedom, they taught me to stand in faith, to look beyond my own pain and access the love, faith and peace to stand for another. God doesn't build with human wisdom. He is an expert builder, wiser than my own understanding. He is a genius. The way He went about healing the foundations in my own life were to give me the access and green light to help another. With each victory we celebrate the victory is His. I made it through each of the internal conflicts and battles that I faced and we won, together. Today I know who I am, I am His.

With each step of the process I grew stronger in Him. Yes, I was saved the day I invited Jesus into my heart, however there were many victories to overcome. I needed to know the love of Jesus, the love of a Daddy and the love of the Holy Spirit. These three revelational truths learnt daily through experience, took me into the kingdom reality and experience. At the forefront of each victory is the revelational truth that I belong to Daddy God and nothing would or could snatch me from Him ever again. I was safe, I am safe. Each day I feed on these basic revelational truths. As I look back I see victory after victory after victory and I smile. Today when I reflect on the years gone by, terror no longer haunts me. Love overtook the darkness, because the darkness could not stand, the darkness was a lie. My job in this process was to not believe the lie, to continue to reject the lie. It lost its power when I refused to listen, when I refused to believe it. My Daddy God's word is truth, my daddy is bigger, He is stronger, He is love, we win.

I recall in this season witnessing miracle after miracle. One time there was a guest speaker at our church and he was very focused on the administration of the Kingdom of heaven invading earth and he walked in the gift of healing. During the conference I noticed that there was a little boy who was in a wheel chair. I heard the Holy Spirit whisper to my heart, please pray for him. I was a bit surprised and not sure how to go up to his mum and ask permission to pray. I waited, I waited for wisdom. The next day I heard the same prompt in my heart. Again I wasn't sure how to do it. I confirmed with the Spirit that he wanted me to do it. It was a directional word. Again I waited. The last day of the conference was the third day and I was standing at the back of the meeting and I noticed that there were people talking with the family. I knew it was now or never. I walked over to the child who had his family with him, mum and dad were close. I politely asked if I could pray. Dave was near me, so I asked if he would pray with me. He agreed. I got on my knees and looked up at this beautiful little man staring at me. I introduced myself and asked him to tell me his name. Caleb, his smile was massive. I said 'Caleb can you give me a high five?', putting my hand up in easy reach. He slapped it hard. I said 'Caleb, I'm going to ask daddy God to give you a high five.' He gave a little giggle. I asked if we could pray and if that was ok. He agreed. Dave and I said a simple prayer releasing the presence of God over him. It was obvious that He was receiving, it was beautiful to see. Caleb was about nine at the time. The medical team that were treating Caleb said that he would never walk, he never had and he never will. About five minutes later I asked how Caleb was feeling. He said good. Dave then politely interjected and said 'Caleb do you want to walk?' Dave taught me a valuable lesson that day: pray, believe and test it. Caleb started unlocking the buckle that held him in the chair. What happened next shocked everyone. Caleb stood and took several steps unaided! Dave and I grabbed him by either hand. Dave asked 'Do you want to walk with us?' His face was beaming with joy. His mum was crying, tears of love, tears of joy. We walked around the church. Dave and I either side, my heart was screaming on the inside and it came though. I was yelling 'Yes!...Yes!...Yes! I couldn't believe what I was witnessing, a little boy defying medical science. They said that he would never walk, yet he did. I saw it with my own eyes, we all did. I could feel the strength grow in Caleb's legs with each step we took. Everyone was looking at Caleb walking and there was much celebration. God showed up and He showed off. It was awesome to see and such an honour to be a part of. My faith continued to grow. I thanked God for that directional word. It took me three days to sum up the courage to do it, but I did. I learnt how obedience is powerful and really important.

A few weeks later there was a row of people that had come forward at the alter at church for prayer. I was a part of the prayer team and felt led to go up to Kevin. Kevin was a father figure in the church, a beautiful man who I and many others have great respect for. I asked him why he was there for prayer, what his need was? He disclosed that he had prostate cancer. This tugged at my heart strings having lost a dad to cancer many years earlier. I had secretly prayed to God to make the enemy suffer for taking my dad early. Watching him die of cancer was one of the hardest things that I had ever experienced. Behind closed doors I asked God for the anointing to see people delivered from cancer. These thoughts flashed through my mind in what felt like a millisecond. He had no idea of my thoughts or my history. I started to pray, releasing the Glory over him, the presence of God. Clearly I heard: 'Healed in Jesus name.' I could see the presence of God all over him and he was drinking it in. He is a man who loves God. Confidently I said to Kevin. 'You have been healed in Jesus name.' He smiled and agreed believing what I had said. I told him 'That's what I heard in the spirit.' Kevin came up to me about a week later and said 'I got my test results back and I have been healed of cancer. No cancer showed up in the recent tests!' I was so excited. Yay! God healed him. God reinforced through this experience how He loves to invade the impossibilities that we face. Six years later I was at a function and Kevin was there also and I asked: 'how have you been, cancer free?' He said 'Yes it never did return - to this day I have remained free of cancer.' Again we celebrated God's faithfulness. My heart leapt with happiness. The victories are so sweet. I stop and I enjoy them. I remind myself regularly of the experiences that I have had and the things I have seen with my own eyes. I have seen the impossibilities become possible, not just with my life, but in the lives of many others.

Courage Over Adversity

IN THE SHELTER OF HIS WINGS

You said be still and know that I am God
As I quite my soul, my mind, my heart finds rest
I distance myself from the world
No one can touch me here; I'm protected, peaceful and safe
The chaos, the stress of life continues as if I was non existent
But it can't sweep me away; nothing is going to distract me from here   I hide in the shelter of His wings, His sanctuary
Here I find refuge, strength, security and trust
to continue on the narrow road
As he speaks His truth into my heart
His word breathes courage and strength to face tomorrow
The world just don't get it they don't understand
How does MY FUTURE fit together?
My God He knows
I trust...., I stand.... I kneel...I surrender...
I lay it all down
Whatever happens, my God He has me in the palm of His hand

I allow His embrace to restore my weariness
His heart beat drums faith, understanding and wisdom
One touch of His garment brings restoration and healing
His story is complete
The miraculous, yes, I believe in miracles
The chapters outline the sanctification process
His faithfulness is evident
My weakness shows his POWER
My life speaks of unconditional love
The Heart Beat of my Father

Courage Over Adversity

During this next season I had an experience that is etched into the foundations of my life. It was an important life lesson from the voice of the Spirit, Daddy to daughter. One day I was walking through a park in the city and something grabbed my attention. I sensed I was to stop, sit and wait. I didn't understand this urge to sit, but I was obedient and sat on a nearby bench beside a pond. Some stringy plants and a few lilies floated on top but the pond was so murky I couldn't see the bottom. I sat there thinking, 'Okay, what's this about?' My mind was still in 'doing' mode even though I felt constrained to sit. I stared blankly into the brown water, pondering whether any life could exist down there. At that moment I saw the outline of a fin. A large orange goldfish slowly made its way to the surface and was joined by another one, white this time. A childlike excitement rose in me as a turtle poked its head above the surface. I giggled and said, 'Hello'. The more I peered into the water, the more my perspective was changed. I was now seeing the many life forms in that pond clearly. Rocks of different sizes, various plants and schools of small fish were revealed. I was getting the message: we put ourselves under such pressure to perform, to achieve, but if we allow ourselves to be still we will hear the quiet voice of the Holy Spirit guiding and giving new perspective and insight. It was time to see and hear that He was saying we were moving into a greater level of unity over the next years. I had to depend on His word every day to teach, guide and direct my steps. I entered into a deeper level of relationship and was eager to speak to Him each day, and seek His heart for myself and others.

Deliverance from my past continued for many years. Step by step my soul recovered from the trauma that we faced as a family, the effects of living under a curse. As the experience of heaven touched my soul, Daddy God would take me deeper into intimacy with Him. During those years my life bore much fruit, I was led by the Spirit to help others, to visit psychiatric hospitals, to care for the broken, to travel overseas and to care for the poor. To preach the good news and share my story with many young people, as well as having the privilege of leading many into the heart of Jesus.

A friend of mine was a scripture teacher in a public school. I would regularly volunteer my time, helping her out for lunch time programmes and camps. I would also go into the classes and talk about my testimony, sharing honestly about my experiences in the occult. Many teenagers are searching for a 'spirituality' and find themselves caught up in the new Age with its consequences. Susan believed it was important to teach the students about the consequences of fooling around with spiritual practices. She became aware that one of her students was facing an incredible amount of difficulty, suffering panic attacks and anxiety after she connected online to a ouija board. Her parents and her doctor were close to admitting her to a psychiatric hospital.

Laura had been exploring her spirituality and was searching online one night and found the Ouija board. Most often the spirits who are contacted through the Ouija are those who reside on the 'demonic astral plane'. I believe this is an incredibly dangerous experience to connect to and has the ability to create chaos in your life. This decision to play around with the spiritual realm came at a great cost for Laura. She learnt first-hand that it is an incredibly dangerous thing to do, even if it doesn't mean anything to you at the time, and seems like a bit of innocent fun. It is a decision that will place you in a place of serious vulnerably and may have catastrophic consequences, possibly similar to mine or worse.

Laura found herself in deep waters, with experiences that were hard for many to understand. She would see things, doors would slam, she would feel a choking feeling around her throat. In the dark hours of the night a spirit would harass, spook and terrify her. She thought she was losing her mind. They were supernatural experiences that were hard to explain and when she did, the people closest to her thought that she was going crazy. The doctor's solution was to place her on a mild anti-depressant and Laura was very close to being admitted to hospital in a psych ward. She was in a fearful state and did not know what to do. Most of the experiences were happening at night. She became extremely distressed at night and was having very little sleep. Thankfully she had an understanding Scripture teacher who was aware of these types of experiences and believed it was real. She understood that there was a way out. Susan was aware of my story, which she shared with Laura and she offered Laura the opportunity for me to come in and talk with her. Laura agreed.

Laura was a small and very skinny teenager and sat in the corner of the room. It was obvious by her appearance that she was struggling. She was pale and looked stressed out. I sat down on the floor besides her and encouraged her to share her story with me. I reassured her that 'things like this can happen.' I also said: 'many will think you have lost your mind!' I could see the relief on her face, she told me she felt reassured that someone understood her struggle. She explained her experiences and talked about the anxiety and panic that it was causing. I explained to her that she had opened a door in the spiritual realm, and there was a way of closing it. I gave her insight about the different realms, good and evil. With Ouija, evil lived behind those doors. Reassuring her that God, our Dad, has all authority over all realms, and had the ability to shut the doors permanently, was important for her to know. Laura had given her life to Jesus previously but had not really walked in the fullness of that decision. I explained that Jesus was the answer and it was in His name that these doors would close. Then I saw a picture of Jesus standing knocking at a door and told her what the Holy Spirit was showing me. I gave her the choice, saying 'Jesus is wanting to come and help out. 'It's your decision. Do you want him to come into your heart?' I was led to explain to her the importance of Jesus in this process and to clearly explain that the demonic has to listen to Jesus. Jesus holds the key to life and death, to open and to shut these doors. It was a decision that was life changing for the good. She said 'yes I do, I want Jesus to come into my heart, I want to do it.' I took her through a simple prayer, inviting Jesus into her heart, confessing Him as Lord. We then went on to ask for him to help out with the situation with the dark spiritual door that was open. I asked her to renounce her connection to this spirit and then I prayed over her. Led by the Spirit, I broke off any connection with this evil. I took authority over it and covered her with the love of Jesus. I could see the Holy Spirit all over her. She started to glow, light flooded her, the demonic spirit left and she was free. The next week she confirmed that life returned to normal and that spirit was no longer harassing her. Two weeks later she was invited by Susan and I to share her story with the rest of the group. She warned the students of the risk of playing around with spiritual experiences, particularly ouija boards.

I felt so honoured to be a part of this experience. It made my suffering a little bit sweet. I saw how our mess gives us a powerful message. I was able to intervene in the plans of darkness. To stop it dead in its tracks as it tried to destroy this young life. I thanked the Holy Spirit for His invitation, to be a part of this dramatic turnaround, this kid's freedom. I celebrated the victory with Susan and I continued to work with her in her scripture class and lunch time group.

*The Spirit of the Sovereign LORD is on me
Because the LORD has anointed me
to proclaim good news to the poor.
He has sent me to bind up the brokenhearted,
to proclaim freedom for the captives
and release from darkness for the prisoners,
to proclaim the year of the LORD'S favour
Isaiah 61:1-2*

ANGIE AMUSO

THE MOUNTAIN

The mountain
Will I make it?
Man this is tough
All the preparation, training
couldn't prepare
The unexpected
My only protection...
The guide rope, connected to Heaven
I sensed Heaven willing me to the top
With every incline, I faced a new test of my stamina, endurance and ability
Every muscle stretched; I'm at my capacity What feels beyond its limits
Hearts racing
Breathe
Believe
There isn't a choice
Determination, focus and will Strengthens the mind
My journey
My responsibility

Courage Over Adversity

Courage
A whole lot of help from my friend
He believes in me
Momentum takes over
The slip stream
Grace...Success...Victory...
Yes, I conquered that mountain
Feels great.

Fast forward a few years. I was talking to a friend who was a volunteer at a mental health hospital in Adelaide. One of the hospitals that I had been a patient in on many occasions. She informed me that this hospital embraced natural therapies. I was instantly alert and asked her what that looked like. She explained that there were volunteers at the hospital administrating Reiki energy to patients on a weekly basis. I was furious! The very practice that had brought me close to death was being offered to psychiatric patients! I was greatly concerned for them, knowing that Reiki could push them over the edge into a spiritual chasm they may not recover from. I knew I needed to act quickly.

In a letter to the Director of Health at the hospital I shared my concerns. I described my personal experiences with Reiki and expressed deep concern for the patients in their care. Usually ex-mental health patients just live a mediocre life and carry the shame of the mental health stigma. Not me. I had to overcome that type of thinking. I refused to let it box me in.

I posted the letter and prayed my heart out. I was deeply distressed about this matter. A week later I received a letter informing me that the hospital was unaware that Reiki had been offered to their patients. The authorities thanked me and said that they would have a meeting about it and get back to me.

A few weeks later, a letter from the director of the hospital arrived, informing me that Reiki had now been accepted as part of the policy within the hospital, and that official permission had been given for Reiki to be administered to psychiatric patients. I was devastated. I complained to God, 'This is not right!' I questioned my position in the community and my role in this matter. A war started in my head: who do you think you are? I know who I am. I'm heaven's kid! I also knew that sometimes God allows conflict in order to effect change. This was such a time.

The burden of what was happening in this hospital to its psychiatric patients was so heavy on my heart. I can tell you it was not comfortable at all. I tried to shrug it off, I tried to suppress it. I rejected it. But it wouldn't move. God made sure it stayed. It was His way of saying that I needed to act.

I began to understand it was our joint concern. I thought... Really? Me? And I sensed God smiling. The pain of caring about this was real and He wasn't about to lift it off me. In my spirit I said 'Right, this situation is not okay. This isn't about me. This is war, a love war, and God wins!' So I prayed and I prayed and still the burden did not lift. I prayed some more. I couldn't do anything but think about the burden that was sitting in my heart. I said, 'God why is this?'

I felt led to go to the beach. I sat on a fence and started praying in faith. In a little while a person I knew slightly came up the path in the company of a lady I did not know. My friend introduced her as a Reiki Master. I knew this meant she was a fully qualified Reiki healer. I joined the dots. This was no coincidence. I decided to risk asking her a question. 'Can you tell me: is it good practice to administer Reiki energy into a psychiatric patient's body?' She replied that it was not wise to do Reiki on people who were dealing with psychological trauma. She said it could lead to psychotic episodes and further psychiatric issues.

In my heart I started celebrating. I knew she was the answer to my prayer. I had a long conversation with her about Reiki and I hugged her when I said goodbye. Healing was taking place in my life. I had faced my fears by talking with her. I gained strength to fight for what was truth and advocate for the spiritually poorest people in the community. They needed to be protected from the policy that had allowed Reiki into that hospital and placed them at risk of further damage. I had known that was the case, but now a Reiki Master had confirmed it.

I rewrote my letter to the hospital director and sent copies to various departments, with a formal complaint about the new policy. I explained that I had researched the Reiki energy and spoken to leading professionals in the industry and they too shared my concerns about Reiki being administered to the patients. I repeated my personal experience and concern. A short time later I received an email thanking me for my letter and explaining that Reiki energy had ceased to be administered to psychiatric patients at that facility. It was no longer an accepted policy. The volunteer at the hospital confirmed that Reiki energy healing sessions had been canceled. The burden in my heart was instantly lifted.

I allowed myself to be quietly pleased at this victory and rejoiced that justice had prevailed. And I understood that my foolish ignorance many years before had laid the groundwork for this victory. Truly, 'He takes our mess and gives us a message.'

CONCLUSION

My story highlights His glory. My present and future highlights HIS STORY, showing His unconditional love, grace, mercy, forgiveness, redemption and restoration. I had seen and heard pain, persecution and grief that took me to the edge of sanity. You will know what I mean if you have been there. Outside of God's grace it's a place of darkness and I didn't want to revisit it. He took me back to it, not to shame me but to show me how great is the victory. Every part of that victory speaks of His power in my weakness. For me, it is so important to minister from a position of victory; to testify from the position of His strength; to bring Him honour.

May my story inspire faith that God does what is impossible. That revelation kept me going when I thought I wouldn't make it, when I felt like giving up and giving in.

Someone out there is depending on your obedience, too.

JESUS

Thank you,
Thank you my Friend
For choosing me
And taking me out
And taking me into...
The ultimate and absolute truth.
I am eternally grateful
My life is not my own any more.
It's different, it's beautiful,
My mind is single and focused
It's all about Him
There is no other choice.

'Nothing is impossible.'

ACKNOWLEDGEMENTS

Special Thanks To:

JESUS - For the price that you paid for my freedom; this is our story and HIS REWARD.

SARAH ROWAN DAHL - Thank you for the book cover your incredible graphics are amazing. Your friendship a gift.

RHONDA POOLEY- The long hours and honesty you put in to editing my book, thank you for being a part of this dream come true.

AVA- Your feedback, encouragement and unconditional love.

DAWN SAWTELL- The lady who refused to give up on me, you loved me with the heart of Heaven, I will always be thankful.

SALLY-ANE AND PETE RAINBOW- You held me close and refused to give up. You entered into my war and believed for my freedom. I will always respect you.

LORRAINE AMUSO- I adore you, you mean the world to me mum.

MARAYANN KNOWLES- My twin the gift of love, the kid that taught me to live in the paradox

JAMES MASON- Photo credit, thank you.

JULIANNE POWELL- for your support, trust and love

SIMON- For your commitment and gift as a publisher

ABOUT ANGIE AMUSO

Angie can be contacted:
my_vision@live.com.au
www.courageoveradversity.com

www.ingramcontent.com/pod-product-compliance
Lightning Source LLC
Chambersburg PA
CBHW022228010526
44113CB00033B/678